BrightRED Study Guide

Curriculum for Excellence

N5

COMPUTING SCIENCE

Alan Williams

BrightRED
PUBLISHING

First published in 2013 by:
Bright Red Publishing Ltd
1 Torphichen Street
Edinburgh
EH3 8HX

A CIP record for this book is available from the British Library

ISBN 978-1-906736-36-1

With thanks to:
PDQ Digital Media, Bungay (layout), Ivor Normand (editorial)
Cover design and series book design by Caleb Rutherford – eidetic

Acknowledgements
Every effort has been made to seek all copyright-holders. If any have been overlooked, then Bright Red Publishing will be delighted to make the necessary arrangements. All Internet links in the text were correct at the time of going to press.

Permission has been sought from all relevant copyright holders and Bright Red Publishing are grateful for the use of the following:

Petr Vaclavek/Shutterstock.com (p 7); koya979/Shutterstock.com (p 11); cobrasoft/Stock-Xchnge (p 13); Stephen Coburn/Shutterstock.com (p 14); jcjgphotography/Shutterstock.com (p 15); giel/Stock-Xchnge (p 16); Konstantin Chagin/Shutterstock.com (p 18); Richard Peterson/Shutterstock.com (p 21); grafvision/Shutterstock.com (p 24); wavebreakmedia/Shutterstock.com (p 25); Stock-Xchnge (p 26); sebleedelisle/CreativeCommons (CC BY 2.0)[1] (p 28); sergign/Shutterstock.com (p 30); 621st Contingency Response Wing/Creative Commons (CC BY 2.0)[1] (p 34); Andi Collington (p 37); Caleb Rutherford (p 44); Labyrinth X/Creative Commons (CC BY-SA 2.0)[2] (p 50); Horia Varlan/Creative Commons (CC BY 2.0) [1] (p 50); cstrom/Creative Commons (CC BY-SA 2.0)[2] (p 52); Argonne National Laboratory/Creative Commons (CC BY-SA 2.0)[2] (p 56); Intel_DE/Creative Commons (CC BY-ND 2.0)[3] (p 57); ionyka/Stock-Xchnge (p 60); Caleb Rutherford (p 60); ffolas/Shutterstock.com (p 61); Pakmor/Shutterstock.com (p 62); Aaron Amat/Shutterstock.com (p 67); Richard Peterson/Shutterstock.com (p 67); Jezper/Shutterstock.com (p 68); bumihills/Shutterstock.com (p 69); gemphoto/Shutterstock.com (p 70); Garsya/Shutterstock.com (p 72); Robin Lund/Shutterstock.com (p 73); Screenshot of 'Flying Toasters' screensaver, After Dark software © Berkeley Systems (p 74); Filip Krstic/Shutterstock.com (p 75); Tatiana Popova/Shutterstock.com (p 75); Stock-Xchnge (p 76); ionyka/Stock-Xchnge (p 82); qwikrex/Creative Commons (CC BY-SA 2.0)[2] (p 82); Aspen Photo/Shutterstock.com (p 82); Victor1558/Creative Commons (CC BY 2.0)[1] (p 84); D.Boyd/Creative Commons (CC BY 2.0)[1] http://creativecommons.org/licenses/by/2.0/) (p 85); Stoppe/Creative Commons (CC0 1.0) (p 87); Ermolaev Alexander/Shutterstock.com (p 88); Robyn Mackenzie/Shutterstock.com (p 89); Andresr/Shutterstock.com (p 90); Ron and Joe/Shutterstock.com (p 90); ostill/Shutterstock.com (p 93).

[1](CC BY 2.0) http://creativecommons.org/licenses/by/2.0/
[2](CC BY-SA 2.0) http://creativecommons.org/licenses/by-sa/2.0/
[3](CC BY-ND 2.0) http://creativecommons.org/licenses/by-nd/2.0/
[4](CC0 1.0) http://creativecommons.org/publicdomain/zero/1.0/

Printed and bound in the UK by Martins the Printers.

CONTENTS

1 THE NATIONAL 5 COURSE

Syllabus and Assessment 4

2 SOFTWARE DESIGN AND DEVELOPMENT

Data Representation 1 6
Data Representation 2 8
Data Types and Structures 10
Programming Constructs 1 12
Programming Constructs 2 14
Programming Constructs 3 16
Design Notations 18
Standard Algorithms 20
Errors in Programs and Readable Code 22
Testing Programs 24
Translation of High-Level Languages 26
Computer Architecture 28
Outcomes and Unit Assessment 30
Questions and Answers 1 32
Questions and Answers 2 34
Questions and Answers 3 36
Questions and Answers 4 38
Questions and Answers 5 40

3 INFORMATION SYSTEM DESIGN AND DEVELOPMENT

Database Structure 1 42
Database Structure 2 44
Websites 46
User Interface 48
Types of Media 50
Factors Affecting File Size 52
Scripting, Mark-up Languages and Testing 54
Types of Computer 56
Input and Output Devices 58
Storage Devices 60
Hardware and Operating System Requirements . . . 62
Computer Networks 64
Security Risks 1 66
Security Risks 2 68
Security Precautions 70
Legal Implications 72
Environmental Impact 74
Outcomes and Unit Assessment 76
Questions and Answers 1 78
Questions and Answers 2 80
Questions and Answers 3 82
Questions and Answers 4 84
Questions and Answers 5 86

4 COURSE ASSESSMENT

The Coursework Task 88
The Exam 90
Guidance and Advice 92

5 GLOSSARY 94

SYLLABUS AND ASSESSMENT

INTRODUCTION

The main purpose of this book is to improve your chances of success in the National 5 Computing Science course. The knowledge required for the exam and unit assessments is provided clearly and concisely. The book is intended not to cover wider issues beyond the syllabus but to present you with revision materials in a summarised version that target the requirements of the exam. Regularly studying this book will go a long way towards your success in this course.

SYLLABUS

This course is made up of three units:

1   Software Design and Development

2   Information System Design and Development

3   Course Assessment

The first two units are mandatory and provide the content on which the course assessment is based.

An outline of the contents of each unit is given in the tables below.

Software Design and Development	
Data representation	Positive numbers, integers and real numbers, characters, graphics (bit-mapped and vector), instructions
Data types and structures	Variables, integer, real, string, Boolean 1-D arrays
Programming constructs	Assignment, selection (simple and complex conditional statements), iteration (fixed and conditional loops) Arithmetic operations (+, −, *, /, ^) Logical operators (AND, OR, NOT) Pre-defined functions
Design notations	Pseudocode Graphical design (structure diagrams)
Standard algorithms	Input validation
Testing and documentation	Normal, extreme and exceptional data Syntax, execution and logic errors Readability of code (internal commentary, meaningful identifiers, indentation)
Translators	Translation of high-level program code into machine code with interpreters and compilers
Computer architecture	Processor structure, memory, buses, interfaces

Information System Design and Development	
Structures and Links	Database structure: flat file, linked tables Field types (text, numbers, date, time, graphics, calculated, link, Boolean) Field lengths and range of values Key field Website, page, URL Hyperlinks (internal and external) Navigation
User interface	User requirements, visual layout, navigation, selection, consistency, interactivity, readability Users: expert, novice, age-range
Types of media	Standard file formats for text, audio, graphics, video, spreadsheets, PDF Factors affecting file size and quality, including resolution, colour depth, sampling rate The need for file compression
Coding and testing	Scripting languages (including JavaScript) Mark-up languages (including HTML) Testing

contd

Hardware and software requirements	Input and output devices Processor type and speed (Hz) Memory (RAM, ROM) Operating system Device type (supercomputer, desktop, laptop, tablet, smartphone)
Storage devices	Built-in, external, portable Magnetic, optical Solid state Capacity, speed Rewritable, read-only Interface type and speed
Computer networks	Peer-to-peer, client/server Media: wired, optical, wireless Web/cloud storage
Security risks	Spyware, phishing, keylogging Online fraud, identity theft DOS (Denial of Service) attacks
Security precautions	Passwords/encryption to protect data Biometrics Security protocols and firewalls Use of security suites
Legal implications	Computer Misuse Act Data Protection Act Copyright, Designs and Patents Act (plagiarism) Health and Safety regulations
Environmental impact	Energy consumed by computing equipment Disposal of IT equipment Carbon footprint

DON'T FORGET

You should use the syllabus as a kind of checklist to make sure that you understand exactly what knowledge is required for assessments in this course. Read it through and ask yourself if you know the topics covered in the table.

ASSESSMENT

The course assessment consists of an examination and a practical assignment. More details of the structure of the question paper and the practical assignment are given at the end of this book.

Course Assessment Structure

Component 1   Question Paper 90 marks
Component 2   Assignment 60 marks
Total marks   150 marks

Grades

You will be given an overall grade (A–D) which is based upon your performance in the two components of the course assessment. The grade is calculated from the total of the two marks. A brief description of the standard required to achieve each grade is given below.

Grade A is awarded to students who have produced a consistently high level of performance in the skills, knowledge and understanding of the course.

Grade B is awarded to students who have produced a fairly high performance in the skills, knowledge and understanding of the course.

Grade C is awarded to students who have produced a successful performance in the skills, knowledge and understanding of the course.

Grade D is awarded to students who have not produced a satisfactory performance in the skills, knowledge and understanding of the course.

DON'T FORGET

In addition to your performance in the course assessment, you must also have passed the unit assessments to gain your grade award for this course. The unit assessments are assessed as a pass or fail and do not determine your overall grade, but you must pass them to complete the course.

THINGS TO DO AND THINK ABOUT

Be aware of the marks allocated to the assessments for this course. Don't spend too much time on a component that is not worth many marks at the expense of losing lots of marks in a more important component.

DATA REPRESENTATION 1

BINARY NUMBERS

A computer is a **two-state** device in that it uses electric charges set to two different values (ON or OFF) to store data and program instructions. Just like an electric light bulb, the charge can be represented by a 1 for ON and a 0 for OFF.

The data stored on a computer can be represented by **binary numbers**, which are made up of the two digits 1 and 0. Human beings find it harder to work with binary numbers than with the decimal number system that we are used to for representing numbers and performing calculations.

UNITS

The following units of storage are used to represent the size of files and the capacity of storage devices on computer systems:

A **bit** is a binary digit.	(1 or 0)
A **byte** is a group of 8 bits.	(for example 10111011)
A **kilobyte** (Kb) is 1,024 bytes.	(2^{10} bytes)
A **megabyte** (Mb) is 1,024 kilobytes = 1,048,576 bytes.	(2^{20} bytes)
A **gigabyte** (GB) is 1,024 megabytes = 1,073,741,824 bytes.	(2^{30} bytes)
A **terabyte** (Tb) is 1,024 gigabytes = 1,099,511,627,776 bytes.	(2^{40} bytes)
A **petabyte** (Pb) is 1,024 terabytes = 1,125,899,906,842,624 bytes.	(2^{50} bytes)

There are units of storage larger than a petabyte. Use a search engine to find the names and the capacities of the next three units.

POSITIVE NUMBERS

Positive whole numbers are represented in a computer system in the binary number system. The binary number system uses units of twos, fours, eights, sixteens etc. to represent a number instead of the units of tens, hundreds, thousands etc. used in the decimal system.

For example, the number 155 is represented by 10011011:

EXAMPLE:

128	64	32	16	8	4	2	1		
1	0	0	1	1	0	1	1	= 128 + 16 + 8 + 2 + 1 =	155.

Changing Decimal Numbers to Binary

The method shown here is used to convert a decimal number into binary. The example converts the number 213 into binary.

The number 213 is repeatedly divided by 2 until it is reduced to 0.

Write down the remainders for each division. The remainders (read from bottom to top) give the binary number.
Answer = 11010101.

2	213	
2	106	R 1
2	53	R 0
2	26	R 1
2	13	R 0
2	6	R 1
2	3	R 0
2	1	R 1
	0	R 1

INTEGERS

Integers are numbers which include positive and negative whole numbers and the number zero. The numbers 7, –13, 0, 456, –23 and 673 are all examples of integers. Decimal and fractional numbers such as 3·5, –10·467 and 2¾ are not integers.

A system called **two's complement** is used to represent these numbers in binary on a computer system. This is similar to the system used for positive numbers, but the first bit is used to store (–128) instead of 128.

If the first bit is a 1, then the number is negative. If the first bit is a 0, then the number is positive.

For example, the number –55 is represented by 11010011 in two's complement:

> **EXAMPLE:**
>
> | –128 | 64 | 32 | 16 | 8 | 4 | 2 | 1 |
> |---|---|---|---|---|---|---|---|
> | 1 | 1 | 0 | 1 | 0 | 0 | 1 | 1 |
>
> = –128 + 64 + 16 + 2 + 1 = –45

For example, the number 93 is represented by 01011101 in two's complement:

> **EXAMPLE:**
>
> | –128 | 64 | 32 | 16 | 8 | 4 | 2 | 1 |
> |---|---|---|---|---|---|---|---|
> | 0 | 1 | 0 | 1 | 1 | 1 | 0 | 1 |
>
> = 64 + 16 + 8 + 4 + 1 = 93

ONLINE TEST

Test yourself on numbers in data representation online at www.brightredbooks.net/N5Computing

REAL NUMBERS

Real numbers include positive and negative whole numbers and numbers which have a decimal fraction part. Numbers such as 6·7, –0·0035, 7·0, 89 and 562·37 are all examples of real numbers.

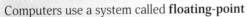

Computers use a system called **floating-point notation** to represent these numbers. A floating-point number is made up of a decimal fraction part called the **mantissa** and a power part called the **exponent**.

> **EXAMPLE:**
>
> Mantissa   Exponent
> ↓   ↓
> $10110110101110101 = 0{\cdot}1011011 \times 2^{10001}$

For example, a floating-point number which uses 16 bits for the mantissa and 8 bits for the exponent is less accurate and stores a smaller range of numbers than a floating-point number that uses 24 bits for the mantissa and 16 bits for the exponent.

Advantage = extremely large and small numbers can be represented in a relatively small number of bits.

Disadvantage = the number is less accurate because the mantissa is rounded off to a set number of significant figures.

DON'T FORGET

The accuracy of a floating-point number is increased by allocating more bits to the mantissa. The range of numbers that can be stored is increased by allocating more bits to the exponent.

DON'T FORGET

Computers use different systems to store different types of numbers. Positive numbers, integers and real numbers are stored as binary numbers, two's complement numbers and floating-point numbers respectively.

THINGS TO DO AND THINK ABOUT

The hexadecimal number system is used in computing as well as the binary number system. Go to the Internet site www.techterms.com and find out why the hexadecimal number system is important in computing.

DATA REPRESENTATION 2

CHARACTERS

Text data is stored in many types of program on a computer. For example, word-processing, databases and websites all require to store textual information. Text is stored on a computer by representing each individual character as a unique binary code. The characters include letters (upper and lower case), numeric digits (0 to 9), punctuation marks (?, &, !, £ etc.) and mathematical operations (+, −, *, / etc.).

ASCII (American Standard Code for Information Interchange)

Standards for text representation have been developed so that different programs using the same codes can interpret data as the same characters.

ASCII is a common standard for representing text that uses an 8-bit (1-byte) code for each character. For example, the letter E is stored as 01000101 (or 69 in decimal), and the character £ is stored as 00100011 (or 35 in decimal).

There are 32 special character codes known as control characters. **Control characters** are special non-printing characters in a character set, used for special purposes. Examples of control characters are Return, Tab and End of file.

The ASCII code system can store 256 different characters.

Unicode

The Unicode system represents each character in a 16-bit (2-byte) code.

ASCII is limited in the number of characters that can be represented (256).

The world has many languages, many of which have different symbols from the English language. The Unicode system was devised to allow the representation of the symbols found in the alphabets of the world in languages such as Japanese, Arabic and so on.

The Unicode system stores each character in 16 bits, which allows $2^{16} = 65,536$ different characters to be represented.

Character Set

A character set is the complete list of characters that a computer system can represent.

This includes uppercase letters, lowercase letters, punctuation symbols, numeric symbols and control characters.

BIT-MAPPED GRAPHICS

The tiny dots that make up a bit-mapped graphic image are called **pixels**. The word 'pixel' comes from the term 'picture element', since the pixels are the elementary parts of a picture.

Bit Depth

A **bit-mapped** graphics program stores the data in a two-dimensional grid of pixels. A binary code is used to represent the colour of each pixel. In a black-and-white image where each pixel can be only two states, black can be represented by a 1 and white by a 0. In an image with lots of colours, several bits are required for the colour code to represent all the different colours. The **bit depth** is the number of bits used for the colour code. Using 24 bits for the colour code of each pixel is quite common, as over 16 million different colours can be represented, which is at the limit of the number of colours that the human eye can distinguish.

Black and White

Colour

contd

DON'T FORGET

The number of bits used to represent the colour of each pixel is called the bit depth. The higher the bit depth, the more colours that can be represented.

Resolution

This is the number of pixels in a fixed area of a bit-mapped graphic.

High-**resolution** images have a large number of small pixels, and low-resolution images have a small number of large pixels.

High-resolution graphics have a better quality than low-resolution graphics but require more storage since there are more pixels in the image.

The resolution of graphics is normally measured in d.p.i. (dots per inch).

VECTOR GRAPHICS

Vector graphics is a type of graphics that stores the image as a collection of objects such as rectangles, circles, lines, triangles and so on. The attributes of each object are stored, such as coordinates, length, breadth, fill colour and so on.

> **EXAMPLE:**
> Circle: centre x, centre y, radius, fill blue, line black and so on.
> Rectangle: start x, start y, length, breadth, fill red, line yellow and so on.
> Line: start x, start y, end x, end y, line red and so on.

COMPARISON OF BIT-MAPPED GRAPHICS AND VECTOR GRAPHICS

There are advantages and disadvantages that each type of graphics program has over others.

	Bit-Mapped Graphics	Vector Graphics
File Size	The file size of bit-mapped graphics is large, since the colour code of thousands or even millions of pixels must be stored.	The file size of vector graphics is generally small, since only the objects and their attributes are stored, not pixels.
Editing	A bit-mapped image is edited at the pixel level.	Vector graphics are edited at an attribute level, for example changing the length of a rectangle or the line colour of a circle. Also, overlapping objects can be separated again, which cannot be done with bit-mapped graphics since the image is not stored as objects.
Fine Detail	Bit-mapped graphics allow the editing of fine detail in photos taken by digital cameras. For example, the program Photoshop uses techniques such as airbrushing to produce the finished photographs shown in magazines, brochures and leaflets.	This kind of fine detail is not possible in vector graphics because the image is made up of shapes such as rectangles and lines.
Enlarging	If a bit-mapped image is enlarged, then it becomes jagged.	The resolution of a vector graphic image is NOT fixed by the resolution of the pixels, so that an enlarged image does NOT become jagged.

 ONLINE

Use a search engine to look up the features of the program Photoshop, using keywords such as 'Photoshop', 'editing', 'basics', 'tutorial' and so on.

 DON'T FORGET

You probably have both types of graphics program on your computer. The graphics program Paint is an example of bit-mapped graphics, whereas the drawing toolbar in Microsoft Word is an example of vector graphics.

 ONLINE TEST

Test yourself on graphics online at www.brightredbooks.net/N5Computing

 THINGS TO DO AND THINK ABOUT

Bit-mapped graphics and vector graphics are two types of graphics software. Each stores and edits the image in different ways. Make sure that you learn the differences and the advantages and disadvantages of each type of software.

DATA TYPES AND STRUCTURES

VARIABLES

Variables are used in programs to store items of data such as a surname, age, exam mark etc. that are entered by the user or produced as the result of a calculation.

A variable is a label given to an item of data so that program instructions can work with them. It is easier to understand programs that use meaningful names for variables, such as Surname, Age and ExamMark and not S, A and E, or – even worse – X, Y and Z.

Most programming languages require the variables used in a program to be declared before they are used.

This makes the program easier to understand by clearly stating which variables are used by the program and also allows the program to set memory aside to store the variables. In a large commercial program, the amount of data stored in variables can be several megabytes.

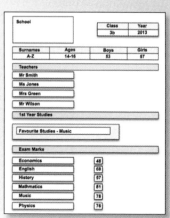

DON'T FORGET

The name given to a variable must not contain any spaces or start with a number. For example, ExamMark is OK but Exam Mark or 1Mark are not allowed.

ONLINE

Check out the tutorial about variables and data types: www.brightredbooks.net/N5Computing

DATA TYPES

A variable such as Surname will hold a piece of text, whereas a variable called Age will hold a number. For this reason, different **data types** are needed to store different kinds of data in programs.

Integers

The **INTEGER** data type is used for a variable that is storing a positive or negative whole number.

> **EXAMPLE:**
> 18, –40, 66, 0, –555, 65,536 and so on.

An INTEGER data type could be used in a program to store an age, the number of people on a bus, the number of a ball in the National Lottery and so on.

Real

The **REAL** data type is used for a variable that is storing a positive or negative decimal number.

> **EXAMPLE:**
> 2·5, 3·14, –5·77, 0, 598·67, 0·00703 and so on.

A REAL data type could be used in a program to store a height, time for a 100m race, weight and so on.

String

The **STRING** data type is used for a variable that is storing an item of text.

> **EXAMPLE:**
> "Violin", "Himalayas", Yes", "Don't walk", "F" and so on.

A STRING data type could be used in a program to store a surname, town, colour and so on.

DON'T FORGET

Schools in Scotland use different languages to teach programming. However, in the exam for this course, the questions on programming code will all be set in a language called Haggis. This book will use Haggis to explain programming concepts.

contd

Boolean

The **BOOLEAN** variable is a two-state variable. It can store either TRUE or FALSE.

> **EXAMPLE:**
> TRUE, FALSE.

A BOOLEAN data type could be used in a program to store an answer to a true-or-false quiz, whether a search item has been found or not, whether an exam mark is a pass or fail, and so on.

Most programming languages use a DIM statement to declare variables.

DIM stands for dimension.

> **EXAMPLE:**
> DIM Age As INTEGER
> DIM Height As REAL
> DIM Surname As STRING
> DIM Found As BOOLEAN

DON'T FORGET

When variables are declared, the name and the data type of each variable is stated.

DATA STRUCTURES

An **array** is an example of a data structure. It is used to store a list of items which are each of the same data type: for example, a list of the names of 20 students in a class, the salary of each employee in a bank, the names of the countries at the Olympics and so on.

Each element of the array can be identified by an index number.

The example below shows a numeric array called Burgers() which is storing a list of six types of burger in a fast-food restaurant.

An index from 0 to 5 is used to identify each element.

Burgers(0)	Burgers(1)	Burgers(2)	Burgers(3)	Burgers(4)	Burgers(5)
Regular	Cheese	Chicken	Double	Mega	Veggie

Arrays must be declared at the start of a program before they can be used. The number inside the brackets specifies how many items the array can store. The data type is stated as String, Integer, Single or Boolean.

Most programming languages use a DIM statement to declare arrays.

DIM stands for dimension.

Examples of arrays of different data types:

> **EXAMPLE:**
> DIM Colours(9) As STRING
> DIM Marks(19) As INTEGER
> DIM Heights(99) As REAL
> DIM Answers(39) As BOOLEAN

DON'T FORGET

An array which is declared as Ages(79) as Integer can store 80 ages and not 79 ages. This is because the array includes an index of 0, so that Ages(0) holds an item of data.

ONLINE TEST

How well do you know data types and structures? Test yourself online at www.brightredbooks.net/N5Computing

THINGS TO DO AND THINK ABOUT

For the main programming language that you use in your school, write down four examples of data types that the language supports. For each data type, use the program's online help to write down the range of values that the data type can be used to represent.

PROGRAMMING CONSTRUCTS 1

INTRODUCTION

Programs are made up of a set of instructions that are executed to solve a problem. The instructions in a program are not simply executed in order from the first instruction to the last instruction. Programs often repeat instructions to improve their efficiency or make decisions by branching to different groups of instructions depending on the value of variables. The order in which the instructions are executed is controlled by three basic constructs. These constructs are called sequence, selection and iteration.

SEQUENCE

Sequencing is when the program executes a list of instructions one after another.

The following program is an example of sequencing. It enters the sides of a cuboid and then calculates and displays the volume of the cuboid. The instructions in this program are executed in sequence one after the other. There is no repetition of instructions or branching within the program.

```
RECEIVE Length FROM KEYBOARD
RECEIVE Breadth FROM KEYBOARD
RECEIVE Height FROM KEYBOARD
SET Volume TO Length * Breadth * Height
SEND ["The volume of the cuboid is: ", Volume] TO DISPLAY
```

This program is an example of Input-Process-Output, where a program enters data, performs a calculation and then displays the result of the calculation. This is essentially how all programs work.

ASSIGNMENT

Variables are used in programs to store items of data. **Assignment** is a term used to describe the process of assigning a value to a variable.

The value assigned to the variable can either be a constant value or the result of a calculation.

EXAMPLE:

The following expression assigns the constant value 20 to the Discount variable.
SET Discount TO 20

EXAMPLE:

The following expression joins a first name and surname together and assigns it to the Fullname variable.
SET Fullname TO Firstname, " ", Surname

EXAMPLE:

The following expression calculates the area of a circle from the radius and assigns it to the Area variable.
SET Area TO 3·14 * Radius ^ 2

contd

ARITHMETIC OPERATIONS (+, –, *, /, ^)

Programming languages perform addition, subtraction, multiplication, division and powers operations. These operations are represented by the symbols shown in the table shown alongside.

Operation	Symbol
Add	+
Subtract	–
Multiply	*
Divide	/
Power	^

The following examples illustrate some uses of these operations:

> **EXAMPLE:**
>
> This instruction calculates the number of pupils in a class.
> SET ClassSize TO Boys + Girls
>
> This instruction calculates an employee's net pay after tax is paid.
> SET NetPay TO Hours * PayPerHour - Tax
>
> This instruction calculates the share of the jackpot that the winners of the National Lottery receive.
> SET Share TO Jackpot / NumberofWinners
>
> This instruction calculates the area of a circle from the radius.
> SET Area TO 3·14 * Radius ^ 2

DON'T FORGET

The symbols '*' and '/' are used in programs to perform multiplication and division.

ONLINE

Check out the online calculator which works out the area of a circle from the radius: www.brightredbooks.net/N5Computing. Can you find another example of an arithmetic operation online?

DON'T FORGET

It is more efficient to use the 'power' symbol than to multiply a variable by itself. For example, Length ^ 3 is more efficient than Length * Length * Length.

COMPARISONS

Programming languages use comparisons such as 'equal to', 'greater than' and so on.

These are represented by the symbols shown in the table alongside.

The following examples illustrate some uses of these operations:

Comparison	Symbol
Equal to	=
Not equal to	<>
Greater than	>
Greater than or equal to	>=
Less than	<
Less than or equal to	<=

DON'T FORGET

The 'greater than or equal to' and the 'less than or equal' to comparisons require two symbols because a keyboard does not have one key to represent this comparison.

> **EXAMPLE:**
>
> This instruction illustrates the 'equal to' comparison.
> IF Age = 5 THEN SEND ["You are old enough to start school."] TO DISPLAY
>
> This instruction illustrates the 'not equal to' comparison.
> IF Age <> 0 THEN SEND ["You have had at least one birthday."] TO DISPLAY
>
> This instruction illustrates the 'greater than' comparison.
> IF Age > 65 THEN SEND ["You should be retired."] TO DISPLAY
>
> This instruction illustrates the 'greater than or equal to' comparison.
> IF Age >= 40 THEN SEND ["Life begins at forty."] TO DISPLAY
>
> This instruction illustrates the 'less than' comparison.
> IF Age < 18 THEN SEND ["You are a child."] TO DISPLAY
>
> This instruction illustrates the 'less than or equal to' comparison.
> IF Age <= 99 THEN SEND ["You are not a century old yet."] TO DISPLAY

ONLINE TEST

Test your knowledge of programming constructs online at www.brightredbooks.net/N5Computing

THINGS TO DO AND THINK ABOUT

Each programming language has different ways of writing the program instructions. Both of the following instructions do the same thing, i.e. they calculate the area of a rectangle. Let Area = Length * Breadth, Let Area := Length * Breadth. Can you think of another two sets of instructions to calculate the area of a circle?

PROGRAMMING CONSTRUCTS 2

SELECTION

Computer programs require to make decisions and execute different sets of instructions depending on the value of variables. For example, a program will take a different action if an exam mark is a pass than if the mark is a fail. The term **selection** describes the process of branching in a program by selecting different sets of instructions to meet the processing demands of different cases.

DON'T FORGET

It is a common mistake to mix up the comparison < with <=. The statement Age < 18 is false when Age is storing the number 18, but the statement Age <= 18 would be true. This is because 18 is not less than 18! The same principle applies to conditions using the comparisons > and >=.

CONDITIONAL STATEMENTS

A **conditional statement** is a statement that is either true or false.

For example, the statement Age < 18 can be either true or false depending upon the value of the variable Age. If Age is storing the number 13, then the statement is true (since 13 is less than 18), but if Age is storing the number 21 then the statement is false (since 21 is not less than 18).

Simple Condition

A simple condition depends upon one conditional statement being true or false.

Programming languages use the IF ... THEN ... ELSE ... END IF construct to execute one set of instructions if a condition is true and another set of instructions if a condition is false. The ELSE part is optional, since sometimes a program requires to perform an action if a condition is true but to do nothing if the condition is false.

This conditional statement illustrates an IF statement without an ELSE.

```
IF Month = 6 THEN SEND ["The month is June."] TO DISPLAY
```

This conditional statement illustrates an IF statement with an ELSE.

```
IF Speed > 30 THEN
    SEND ["Too fast! Slow down."] TO DISPLAY
ELSE
    SEND ["Well done. Nice speed."] TO DISPLAY
END IF
```

Complex Condition

A complex condition depends upon two or more conditional statements being true or false. Programming languages have logical operators (AND, OR, NOT etc.) that can be used to implement complex conditions in program instructions.

DON'T FORGET

It is important to be clear on the difference between the AND and OR logical operators. An AND logical operator means that both of the conditions must be true. An OR operator means that just one of the conditions must be true.

AND

The AND logical operator requires both conditions to be true.

The following IF statement is true only if both of the conditions Sex = "M" AND Age < 18 are true.

```
IF Sex = "M" AND Age < 18 THEN SEND ["You are a boy."] TO DISPLAY
```

contd

OR

The OR logical operator requires one of the conditions to be true.

The following IF statement is true if either Day = "Sat" is true OR Day = "Sun" is true.

```
IF Day = "Sat" OR Day = "Sun" THEN SEND ["It's the weekend!"] TO DISPLAY
```

NOT

The NOT logical operator switches a statement that is false to a statement that is true and vice versa. In other words, if a statement is not false then it is true, or if it is not true then it is false.

The following IF statement is true if Temperature > 0 is false.

```
IF NOT (Temperature > 0) THEN SEND ["It's freezing!"] TO DISPLAY
```

ONLINE

As well as the OR logical operator, there is an EOR logical operator. Use a search engine to investigate the difference between these two operators.

SELECT CASE

Sometimes, when a program requires many IF statements to cover many selections, it is better to use a SELECT CASE construct. This construct allows different instructions to be selected depending on the value of a variable and is more readable than the alternative, which would be using lots of IF statements.

The following example illustrates the use of a SELECT ... CASE ... END SELECT to display an exam grade depending on a percentage mark.

```
SELECT CASE Percentage
CASE 0 To 49
    SEND ["Too bad. You failed!"] TO DISPLAY
CASE 50 To 59
    SEND ["You gained a C pass!"] TO DISPLAY
CASE 60 To 69
    SEND ["You gained a B pass!"] TO DISPLAY
CASE 70 To 100
    SEND ["You gained an A pass!"] TO DISPLAY
END SELECT
```

ONLINE TEST

Test your knowledge of programming constructs online at www. brightredbooks.net/ N5Computing

THINGS TO DO AND THINK ABOUT

Sequencing is when programs execute one instruction after another. However, programs will often use selection, which is when they branch to one or another set of instructions depending on what processing is required for a given situation. Selection can be implemented by using an IF ... THEN ... ELSE ... END IF or a SELECT ... CASE ... END SELECT control construct.

PROGRAMMING CONSTRUCTS 3

ITERATION

Iteration is the process where programs repeat a group of instructions two or more times. Iteration is also known as repetition and looping. Iteration makes programs more efficient by inserting the code to be repeated only once rather than having the same code inserted into the program several times.

FIXED LOOPS

A **fixed loop** is a when a group of instructions is repeated a pre-determined number of times.

The instructions that are to be repeated are placed between the command words FOR ... FROM ... TO ... DO and END FOR. The number of times that the loop is to be repeated is determined by the FOR ... FROM ... TO ... DO command words, which set the start and end value of a loop counter. The END FOR command sets the end point of the instructions that are to be repeated.

The example alongside illustrates the use of a fixed loop to display an address used for labels 6 times. The loop counter (in this case Label_Number) goes from 1 to 6.

```
FOR Label_Number FROM 1 TO 6  DO
    SEND ["Miss S. Candy,"] TO DISPLAY
    SEND ["7 Sugar Crescent,"] TO DISPLAY
    SEND ["Rock City,"] TO DISPLAY
    SEND ["Wyoming,"] TO DISPLAY
    SEND ["U.S.A."] TO DISPLAY
END FOR
```

The example alongside illustrates the use of a fixed loop to display the squares of whole numbers from 0 to 20. The loop counter (in this case Number) goes from 0 to 20.

```
FOR Number FROM 0 TO 20 DO
    SEND [Number ^ 2] TO DISPLAY
END FOR
```

The example alongside shows a fixed loop in the games development program Scratch. This loop is repeated 10 times to perform an animation by changing a costume every tenth of a second.

CONDITIONAL LOOPS

A **conditional loop** is when a group of instructions is repeated until or while a condition is true. An example of a conditional loop is a REPEAT ... UNTIL ... loop. The instructions could be executed only once if the condition is true the first time through the loop, or the instructions could be repeated many times until a condition is true.

Another conditional loop is a WHILE ... DO ... END WHILE loop, which only executes the instructions in a loop while a condition is true. The instructions in the loop might not be executed at all if the condition is not true when first entering the loop.

The following example illustrates the use of a conditional loop where the user is repeatedly asked to guess a mystery number until the user guesses correctly.

```
REPEAT
    RECEIVE Guess FROM KEYBOARD
    IF Guess <> MysteryNumber THEN SEND ["Wrong. Try again!"] TO DISPLAY
UNTIL Guess = MysteryNumber
```

This code could be executed once if the user guesses correctly on the first attempt, but it could be executed many times until the user guesses correctly.

contd

The example alongside shows a conditional loop in the games development program Scratch. A superhero is given three lives, but if he/she touches a baddie then the number of lives is reduced by one. The number of times that the loop is repeated is not fixed but will continue until the number of lives falls to zero.

Nested Loops

A **nested loop** is when one loop is placed completely inside another loop. The loops can be any combination of fixed and conditional loops.

The example alongside is of a nested loop which uses a fixed loop to enter the ages of 12 students and an inner conditional loop to validate that each age is in the range 12 to 18.

```
FOR Student FROM 0 TO 11 DO
    REPEAT
        RECEIVE Age(Student) FROM KEYBOARD
        IF Age(Student) < 12 OR Age(Student) > 18 THEN
            SEND ["The age must be between 12 and 18"] TO DISPLAY
        END IF
    UNTIL Age(Student) > 11 AND Age(Student) < 19
END FOR
```

PRE-DEFINED FUNCTIONS

A function is used in a program to return a single item of data.

A **pre-defined function** is a function already built into the programming language which performs mathematical calculations, manipulates text, formats values and so on. Pre-defined functions can save the programmer a lot of time, since a tried and tested function is available and the code does not need to be written from scratch. Most programming languages have hundreds of pre-defined functions to meet the variety of processing requirements of different application areas.

The Left function returns part of a piece of text. This example returns the first 3 characters from the left of the string, i.e. 'Mac':

```
Left("Macdonald", 3)
```

The Mid function returns part of a piece of text. This example starts at the third character of the string and returns 4 characters, i.e. 'ring':

```
Mid("Meringue", 3, 4)
```

The SQR function returns the square root of a number. This example returns the square root of the value 80:

```
SQR(80)
```

The Format function returns a number in a specified format. This example returns the variable Length, rounded to 2 decimal places:

```
Format(Length, "#·00")
```

ONLINE TEST

Test your knowledge of programming constructs online at www.brightredbooks.net/N5Computing

THINGS TO DO AND THINK ABOUT

The programming languages that you use for your practical work will have their own means of implementing sequence, selection and iteration. The format of the instructions may be different, but they are essentially carrying out the same processing. You should think about when sequencing, selection and iteration are required in your own programs.

DESIGN NOTATIONS

Before a piece of software is written, it goes through the process of design. The design will include a plan of the structure of the program as well as the detailed logic of the program code. It is a mistake to think that design is not necessary and that it would save time to go straight to writing the program code. This approach might be possible for a small-scale program such as a program that finds the average of three numbers. However, in a large commercial project, the design is essential to allow the allocation of sections of code to a team of programmers and to ensure that the program modules work together correctly.

Design notations are diagrams and textual documentation that are used to represent the structure and logic of a program. Structure charts are used for representing the overall picture at a high level, and pseudocode is used for the detail of the programming logic.

DON'T FORGET

The approach here is 'divide and conquer'. It is much easier for a human being to solve several small problems than one large, difficult problem.

STRUCTURE DIAGRAMS

It is much easier for a human being to solve a series of small problems than one large complex problem. A **structure diagram** is used to split a program up into smaller, more manageable parts. This is performed in a series of steps called **stepwise refinement** in which a large problem is broken down into parts and then those parts themselves are further broken down into smaller parts. This process is repeated until the parts are small enough to be easy to solve.

ONLINE

For a summary of the keywords used in Haggis pseudocode, visit www.brightredbooks.net/ N5Computing

A different symbol is used in a structure diagram to make it clear whether sequencing, selection or repetition is taking place.

The different symbols are given below:

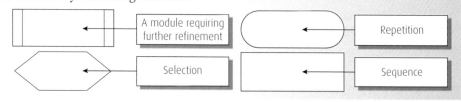

DON'T FORGET

Use everyday language to give the detailed logic of the instruction in pseudocode. Don't use programming keywords. Never write pseudocode such as Let Age = Inputbox("Please enter your age."). Use statements such as RECEIVE Age FROM KEYBOARD or Get Age from user.

PSEUDOCODE

Pseudocode is used at the design stage to represent the detailed logic of the program code. It gives the same detail as the programming code but uses natural language. This allows the logic of the steps required to solve a problem to be produced without worrying about the command words and formatting required of a particular programming language.

Pseudocode shows the design of the programming constructs of sequence, selection and iteration.

DESIGN OF PROGRAMMING CONSTRUCTS

Both structure diagrams and pseudocode can be used at the design stage to illustrate programming constructs.

Sequence

Sequence is where a list of instructions is carried out after another.

contd

The structure diagram alongside shows the sequence of steps required for a program which calculates and displays the area of a rectangle.

The following pseudocode gives the steps required to solve the same problem.

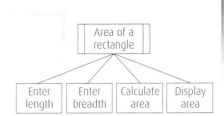

```
1   RECEIVE Length FROM KEYBOARD
2   RECEIVE Breadth FROM KEYBOARD
3   SET Area TO Length * Breadth
4   SEND ["The area is: ", Area] TO DISPLAY
```

Selection

As mentioned previously, selection is where different sets of instructions are carried out depending upon whether a condition is true or false.

The structure diagram alongside shows the steps required for a program which enters the name of a student and an exam mark and gives a message stating whether the mark is a pass or a fail.

The following pseudocode gives the steps required to solve the same problem.

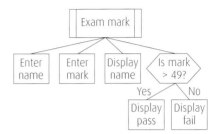

```
1   RECEIVE Name FROM KEYBOARD
2   RECEIVE Mark FROM KEYBOARD
3   SEND [Name] TO DISPLAY
4   IF Mark > 49 THEN
5        SEND ["Pass"] TO DISPLAY
6   ELSE
7        SEND ["Fail"] TO DISPLAY
8   END IF
```

Iteration

Iteration is where groups of instructions are repeated.

The structure diagram alongside shows the steps required for a program which calculates the number of passes and fails in a list of 20 exam marks.

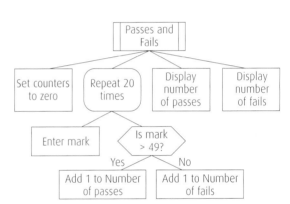

The following pseudocode gives the steps required to solve the same problem.

```
1   SET Passes TO 0
2   SET Fails TO 0
3   REPEAT 20 TIMES
4        RECEIVE Mark FROM KEYBOARD
5        IF Mark > 49 THEN
6            SET Passes TO Passes + 1
7        ELSE
8            SET Fails TO Fails + 1
9        END IF
10  END REPEAT
11  SEND ["The number of passes is: ", Passes] TO DISPLAY
12  SEND ["The number of fails is: ", Fails] TO DISPLAY
```

The following pseudocode displays the numbers in a list of 12 numbers that are under 10.

```
1   SET NumberList TO [12, 3, 8, 16, 24, 4, 17, 5, 11, 6, 15, 18]
2   FOR Index FROM 0 TO 11 DO
3        IF NumberList(Index) < 10 THEN
4            SEND [NumberList(Index)] TO DISPLAY
5        END IF
6   END FOR
```

 ONLINE TEST

Test your knowledge of design notations online at www.brightredbooks.net/N5Computing

 THINGS TO DO AND THINK ABOUT

Structure diagrams and pseudocode can both be used to illustrate the design of a program. There is not only one correct answer to the design of a program, but it is essential that your design shows all of the essential steps and any selection or iteration that is required. Illustrate the design of a program that you have written recently, both in a structure diagram and with pseudocode.

STANDARD ALGORITHMS

INTRODUCTION

Many algorithms are used in programs over and over again. These are called **standard algorithms** or common algorithms. For example, finding the maximum value could be used in a program to find the highest exam mark in a group of students, the longest jump in a long-jump competition, the hottest day in a month of temperatures, and so on. All of these examples are using the same algorithm, and it is important to know standard algorithms so that you can implement them in your own programs.

Most programmers will have a module library of pre-written standard algorithms so that these can be inserted into the program without the need to write the code from scratch.

INPUT VALIDATION

ONLINE

For more information on input validation, visit www.brightredbooks.net/N5Computing

Most programs require the user to enter data from the keyboard. It is very easy for the user to make a mistake and enter data that is not possible. **Input validation** is where the program repeatedly asks for an item of data to be entered until it is within the possible range of values. For example, a month is entered until it is in the range 1 to 12.

When data is entered that is not possible, an error message should give the user feedback on their mistake.

The input-validation algorithm is an example of a conditional loop.

Shown below is pseudocode for an input-validation algorithm.

DON'T FORGET

You should learn this pseudocode as a template solution for input validation. All that needs to change for different input validations is the name of the variable and the values between which it must lie. For example, validating that a month is in the range 1 to 12 would still require the same 6 lines of logic. However, the Percentage variable would be replaced with Month. The numbers 0 and 100 would be replaced with 1 and 12 in line 3, and the numbers –1 and 101 would be replaced with 0 and 13 in line 6.

```
1   REPEAT
2       RECEIVE Value FROM KEYBOARD
3       IF Value is not in range THEN
4           SEND ["Not possible. Try again!"] TO DISPLAY
5       END IF
6   UNTIL Value is in range
```

The particular example of input validation shown below enters and validates a percentage mark so that it is in the range 0 to 100.

```
1   REPEAT
2   RECEIVE Percentage FROM KEYBOARD
3       IF Percentage < 0 OR Percentage > 100 THEN
4           SEND ["Not possible. Try again!"] TO DISPLAY
5       END IF
6   UNTIL Percentage > –1 AND Percentage < 101
```

ONLINE TEST

Test your knowledge of standard algorithms online at www.brightredbooks.net/N5Computing

Apart from data being validated to be in a certain range of values, it can also be validated to be a certain length. For example, a date of birth can be validated to only be accepted if it is 6 digits long: 120656 and so on. Data can also be validated to be of a certain type. For example, a number must be entered and not a letter.

COUNTING OCCURRENCES

This algorithm is used to count the number of times the items in a list of values meet certain criteria: for example, how many surnames in a list start with 'Mac' or how many 100m times in a race are less than 10 seconds.

FINDING THE MAXIMUM VALUE AND THE MINIMUM VALUE

These algorithms are used to find the highest and the lowest value in a list of values. The maximum-value algorithm could be used to find the highest mark in French exam or the worst score in a golf competition. The minimum-value algorithm could be used to find the smallest height of students in a class or the best time in a 400m race.

DON'T FORGET

The maximum value in a list of scores is not always the best value. The best time in a 100m race is the minimum value, not the maximum value. Think carefully whether you require the maximum or the minimum value in a given situation.

LINEAR SEARCH

This algorithm is used to search for an item in a list of values. The list is searched by starting at the first item, then the second item, then the third item and so on until the search value is found or the end of the list is reached.

Searching for a name in a telephone directory or searching for an item in a stock file are examples of linear searches.

There are other standard algorithms apart from the ones listed here. Enter the keywords 'standard algorithm' and 'pseudocode' into a search engine to investigate further examples and what they are used for. For example, a binary search is commonly used in programs.

 THINGS TO DO AND THINK ABOUT

You are expected to know the pseudocode for the input-validation algorithm, and you should also be able to implement this algorithm in your programs.

Write down three examples of data that can be validated to lie within a certain range of values, and give the range of values.

ERRORS IN PROGRAMS AND READABLE CODE

ERRORS

Most programs have errors which have to be detected and removed by testing. There could be errors in the spelling of command words, or errors generated when the program is run, or the program could run to completion but give the wrong results.

There are three types of errors found in programs. These are called syntax, execution and logic errors.

Syntax Errors

These are errors which result from mistakes in the use of the programming language. **Syntax errors** are identified and reported by the translator program when the program is translated.

Syntax errors can take the form of misspelt command words, missing brackets, misplaced commas and so on.

Shown below are some examples of syntax errors in the Visual Basic programming language.

Misspelt language keywords	Inpot, Nxt I, Repeet
Missing brackets	Let Score = InputBox("Enter your score."
Missing inverted commas	Let Colour = "Scarlet.

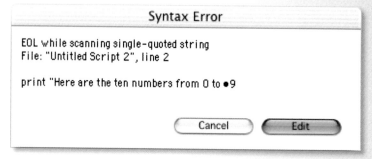

```
Syntax Error

EOL while scanning single-quoted string
File: "Untitled Script 2", line 2

print "Here are the ten numbers from 0 to ●9

                          Cancel        Edit
```

Execution Errors

Even if there are no syntax errors, the program can still produce errors when it is run. **Execution errors** are errors that are detected during the running of the program.

A common execution error is to divide by zero, which is not mathematically possible and causes an error.

Logic Errors

Sometimes, a program can run to completion without crashing or any sign of a problem. However, it could be that there are mistakes in the code that cause errors in the calculations, and the program does not produce the correct results.

These are errors in the logic of the code itself: for example, writing code to add two numbers instead of multiplying them, or subtracting two numbers the wrong way round.

Shown below are two examples of **logical errors**. Both of these instructions would be executed without the program crashing, but they would produce a logic error in the code.

```
'Find the volume of the cuboid
Let Volume = Length + Breadth + Height
```

This instruction is supposed to calculate the volume of a cuboid. By ADDING the length,

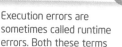

DON'T FORGET

Execution errors are sometimes called runtime errors. Both these terms mean the same thing.

contd

breadth and height, it will give the wrong result, since it should be MULTIPLYING the sides of the cuboid.

```
'Find the range of scores from highest to lowest
Let Range = MinScore - MaxScore
```

This instruction is supposed to find the range of values between a highest and a lowest score. By subtracting the highest score from the lowest score, it gives an error, since it should be subtracting the lowest score from the highest score.

ONLINE

For more on programming errors visit: www.brightredbooks.net/N5Computing

READABLE CODE

A **readable** program is a program that is easily understood by another programmer.

Programs are made readable by using techniques that include inserting internal commentary, or using meaningful variable names and indentations.

It is important that programs are readable so that they can be easily understood and updated in the future.

Internal Commentary

Programming languages allow the programmer to insert comments to explain what the instructions are doing. This is known as **internal commentary**. The comments are not executed when the program is executed but are only there to help a programmer make sense of the program code.

Meaningful Identifiers

Variable names are the labels a programmer gives for items of data used by the program. It is important to choose **meaningful identifiers** that relate to the data in a meaningful way. Variable names such as BestScore and WorstScore make it much easier to understand the program code than variable names such as B and W.

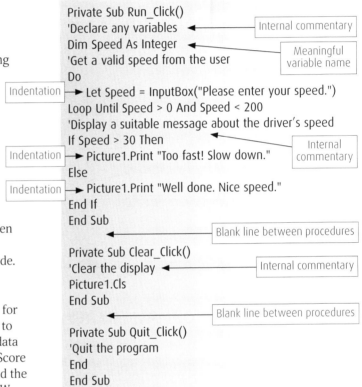

```
Private Sub Run_Click()
'Declare any variables          ◄── Internal commentary
Dim Speed As Integer            ◄── Meaningful variable name
'Get a valid speed from the user
Do
   Let Speed = InputBox("Please enter your speed.")   ◄ Indentation
Loop Until Speed > 0 And Speed < 200
'Display a suitable message about the driver's speed
If Speed > 30 Then
   Picture1.Print "Too fast! Slow down."   ◄ Indentation / Internal commentary
Else
   Picture1.Print "Well done. Nice speed."  ◄ Indentation
End If
End Sub
                                ◄── Blank line between procedures
Private Sub Clear_Click()
'Clear the display              ◄── Internal commentary
Picture1.Cls
End Sub
                                ◄── Blank line between procedures
Private Sub Quit_Click()
'Quit the program
End
End Sub
```

Indentation

Indentation and blank lines between subprograms help to give the program listing a structure so that it is easier to read. This makes it easier to identify the control constructs in the code, such as which sections of code are repeated and which instructions are selected for execution in an IF ... THEN ... ELSE ... END IF construct. Blank lines between procedures make it easier for a programmer to identify where each subprogram starts and ends.

Example of a Readable Program

The example above illustrates how a program can be made more readable by using internal commentary, meaningful variable names, and indentation and blank lines between procedures. The example is given in the Visual Basic programming language.

ONLINE TEST

Test yourself on errors in programs and readable code online at www.brightredbooks.net/N5Computing

THINGS TO DO AND THINK ABOUT

Programs can have different types of error. In the future, if your program fails to produce the correct results, try to identify whether you are correcting syntax, execution or logical errors.

TESTING PROGRAMS

INTRODUCTION

The purpose of testing is to detect and remove errors in a program. Many programs are released onto the market which contain errors that have not been identified at the testing stage by the software development company. In a large program, it is not practical to test the program for all the possible combinations of **test data**; however, it is important to test that the software can cope with as many cases as possible. Programs should be comprehensively tested to see whether they give the correct results when dealing with normal everyday data, extreme data which lies on the boundaries and exceptional data which is outwith the expected limits.

DON'T FORGET

Sometimes, extreme data is referred to as boundary data. Both of these terms mean the same thing, which is test data that is on the limits of normal data.

NORMAL, EXTREME AND EXCEPTIONAL TEST DATA

Programs are not tested in a makeshift, random fashion. A program should be tested methodically with **normal data**, **extreme data** and then **exceptional data** to make sure that it gives correct results when dealing with as many scenarios as possible.

Normal

One set of test data should be chosen to test that the software gives correct results for everyday data which is within the expected range of values.

For example, if a program is entering a percentage mark, then normal data could be 72 and 45.

Extreme

One set of test data should be chosen to see whether the software can handle data which lies on the boundaries of possible data.

For example, if a program is entering a percentage mark, then extreme data could be 0 and 100.

Exceptional

One set of test data should be chosen for extreme cases to test whether the software can deal with unexpected data without crashing.

For example, if a program is entering a percentage mark, then extreme data could be 199, −40, Yes, G12 and so on.

ONLINE

What percentage of the time in software development do you think is spent on testing? Use a search engine to get an estimate of the percentage time, using keywords such as 'software development', 'testing', 'percentage' and so on. You might be surprised by the answer.

EXAMPLES OF TESTING

A program prompts the user to enter the exam marks of 6 students as a percentage. The program then displays the number of students who achieved each of the following grades. (A grade is 70 to 100, B grade is 60 to 69, C grade is 50 to 59, Fail is 0 to 49.)

The program also validates that the entered marks are in the range 0 to 100.

Shown below is an example of how to test a program by first of all choosing the test data with reasons for your choice and then working out the expected results on paper. The test data can then be entered into the program on the computer to see whether it gives the same results as those that have been manually calculated.

The following are examples of normal, extreme and exceptional test data that could be used to test this program. A reason is given for choosing each set of test data, together with the expected results.

Normal test data	56, 32, 66, 89, 62, 43
Reason for choice	This data has been chosen to see whether the program gives correct results for everyday marks that give a mixture of A, B and C grades and fails.
Expected results	A grades 1, B grades 2, C grades 1, Fails 2
Extreme test data	60, 0, 70, 100, 49, 50
Reason for choice	This data has been chosen to see whether the program gives correct results for marks that lie on the boundaries of the grades.
Expected results	A grades 2, B grades 1, C grades 1, Fails 2
Exceptional test data	199, –66, X, £, 7?, cat
Reason for choice	This data has been chosen to see whether the program gives correct results for marks that are not valid percentage exam marks.
Expected results	The program should give an error message and ask for valid marks to be entered.

ONLINE TEST

For a testing test (on testing), go to www. brightredbooks.net/ N5Computing

DON'T FORGET

When testing your own programs, it is important to give a reason for choosing your test data and not just the test data itself. You should also work out on paper the expected results that the program should give with the test data. This is called a dry run.

THINGS TO DO AND THINK ABOUT

Testing program code is not just a topic for the theory questions in the exam. You must also make sure that you comprehensively test your own programs in your practical work by supplying normal, extreme and exceptional test data.

Look at the last three programs that you have written. Write down a set of normal, extreme and exceptional data to test each program. Try out each program with the sets of test data.

TRANSLATION OF HIGH-LEVEL LANGUAGES

MACHINE CODE

Machine code is the computer's own programming language, which uses binary codes to represent the program instructions and data.

Machine-code programs are very difficult for humans to write, and it is easy to make mistakes, since all instructions are made up of patterns of 1s and 0s. Writing machine-code programs is very time-consuming, since the instructions are very simple and it requires many of these instructions to do even simple tasks such as working out the average of a small list of numbers. It is also very hard to find and correct errors in machine-code programs.

Shown below is part of a machine-code program.

```
10111001        00110010 0101001
01000010        101110 101010110
11001110        0100110011110011
01010111        1100010110110101
```

HIGH-LEVEL LANGUAGES

In the early days of computing, all programs were written in machine code. **High-level languages** were developed to make the process of software development easier and quicker. Today, almost all software is written in a high-level language.

Shown below is an example of a program written in a high-level language.

The program asks for the name and age of a dog and then displays the equivalent human age.

```
'Declare variables
Dim DogName As String
Dim DogAge As Integer
Dim HumanAge As Integer
'Get the dog data from TextBoxes
Let DogName = Text1.Text
Let DogAge = Val(Text2.Text)
'Calculate the equivalent human age of the dog
If DogAge < 4 Then
    Let HumanAge = DogAge * 7
Else
    Let HumanAge = 21 + 4 * (DogAge - 3)
End If
'Display a suitable message
Picture1.Print "Dog's age: "; DogAge
Picture1.Print "If "; DogName; " was a human he/she
would be "; HumanAge; " years old."
End Sub

Private Sub Command2_Click()
'Clear the display
Picture1.Cls
End Sub

Private Sub Command3_Click()
'End the program
End
```

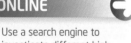
ONLINE

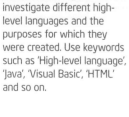
Use a search engine to investigate different high-level languages and the purposes for which they were created. Use keywords such as 'High-level language', 'Java', 'Visual Basic', 'HTML' and so on.

contd

Advantages of High-Level Languages

1   The commands use English keywords such as PRINT, INPUT, REPEAT etc. which are easy to understand and remember.

2   Complex arithmetic can be performed in one instruction that would take many machine-code instructions.
For example: Let Volume = 3·14 * Radius ^ 2 * Height
For example: Let Hypotenuse = SQR(Side1 ^ 2 + Side2 ^ 2)

3   They have inbuilt mathematical and logical functions to process the data.
For example: Let Length = Cos(Angle) * 4
For example: Let Initial = Left(Name, 1)

4   One high-level instruction can perform the same processing as lots of machine-code instructions.

5   The program can be broken down into subprograms (functions and procedures) to produce modular code.

TRANSLATORS

All high-level-language programs must be translated into machine code before they can be run. One high-level-language instruction generally translates into several machine-code instructions.

Compilers

A **compiler** translates the complete program in one go before the program is run.

1   The compiled program runs fast, since there is no translation at run time.
(It has been translated before it is run.)

2   It produces a stand-alone machine-code program which runs by itself without the need for the source code and the compiler.

3   The source program will only be used again if the program needs to be changed.

4   Errors in the source code are only identified when the program is compiled.
Once the errors have been corrected, the complete program has to be compiled again before it can be run and tested.

Interpreters

An **interpreter** translates and executes a program one statement at a time while the program is run.

1   Because the interpreter translates statements as it executes the program (this takes time), it will run more slowly than a compiled program which has been compiled into machine code before it is run.

2   The interpreter must also be in memory as the program is executed, whereas a compiler is not needed once the program has been compiled. Thus an interpreted program requires more memory than the compiled version of the same program.

3   The interpreter has the advantage of being a simpler (and hence less expensive) program.

4   Interpreted programs are easier to edit than compiled programs, since the program will run up to the point of error and can then be corrected and run again immediately, whereas a compiled program requires the complete program to be compiled again before it can be run.

DON'T FORGET

A compiler and an interpreter are two types of programs used to translate high-level languages into machine code. You should know the difference in how each translator operates and the advantages and disadvantages of each.

ONLINE TEST

How well have you learned about the translation of high-level languages? Check online at www.brightredbooks.net/N5Computing

THINGS TO DO AND THINK ABOUT

All computers execute machine code, which is binary patterns that can be executed by a processor chip. High-level languages exist to make it easier for a human to write programs, but a compiler or an interpreter must be used to translate the code into machine code before it can be run.

COMPUTER ARCHITECTURE

COMPUTER SYSTEM

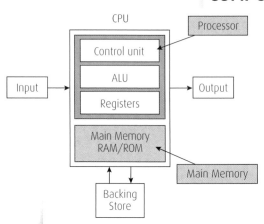

The diagram alongside shows the components of a computer system. All computers work in essentially the same way. Input devices are used to enter data, which is processed by a central processing unit, and then the results are displayed by output devices.

Input is performed by devices such as keyboards, scanners and digital cameras. Output is performed by devices such as flat screens and printers.

The **CPU** (Central Processing Unit) consists of a processor chip and main memory which is made up of RAM and ROM chips.

Backing store devices are used to permanently store programs and data.

Peripheral is a term that is used to describe **input**, **output** and **backing store** devices that are connected to the CPU. Keyboards, USB flash memory and printers are examples of peripheral devices.

DON'T FORGET

Make sure that you know the basic diagram of a computer system and understand the function of the labelled parts.

PROCESSOR

The processor chip has three basic components. These are the control unit, arithmetic logic unit and registers.

Control Unit

The **control unit** manages the execution of program instructions by fetching them one at a time from main memory. The control unit has complex electronic circuits that allow instructions to be decoded and executed. Signals are sent out by the processor to initiate events within the CPU.

Arithmetic Logic Unit

The **ALU** performs arithmetic operations such as addition, subtraction, multiplication and division, and logical decisions such as AND, OR and NOT.

Registers

The processor has individual storage locations called **registers** that temporarily store items of data. For example, the accumulator is a register that stores the results of calculations performed in the ALU. Another processor register is the instruction register, which holds the program instruction that is currently being decoded and executed.

DON'T FORGET

Main memory and backing store are both used to store programs and data on a computer system, but they have very different characteristics. Main memory has much less capacity than backing store and does not store data permanently.

MEMORY

Main memory is used to temporarily store programs while they are being run. It is part of the central processing unit and consists of **RAM** and **ROM** chips.

RAM (Random-Access Memory) can be written to and read from. It loses its contents when power is switched off.

ROM (Read-Only Memory) can be read from but not written to. It does not lose its contents when power is switched off. ROM is used to permanently store programs that are important to the system, such as the BIOS, which loads the operating system from disc when the computer is started up.

When the power is switched off, the data that has been entered into RAM will be lost. Backing store is used to permanently store data that otherwise would be lost.

ADDRESSABILITY OF MAIN MEMORY

Main memory is made up of thousands of millions of storage locations, each of which is used to hold program instructions and data.

Each memory location is given a unique address so that the processor can identify it.

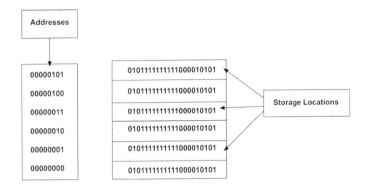

BUSES

A bus is a set of wires used to carry data between the processor and main memory.

Address Bus

The **address bus** is used to specify which memory location is to be used to read data from or to write data to.

Data Bus

The **data bus** is used to carry data from a memory location to the processor and vice versa. It is a two-way bus.

Control Bus

The **control bus** is used to send out signals to initiate events such as reading an item of data from a memory location into the processor or writing an item of data from the processor to a memory location.

ONLINE

Use a search engine to find out other control-bus functions apart from Read and Write.

INTERFACE

An **interface** provides a link between a peripheral device and the CPU and compensates for differences in how they operate.

Differences in Speed

Peripheral devices operate at a much slower speed than the processor. The interface has to compensate for the differences in speed.

Data Storage

Data may be required to be stored temporarily in an area of memory called a buffer until the peripheral device is ready to transfer it.

Data Conversion

Data is often stored in the peripheral device in a different format from how it is stored in the processor. The interface may be required to convert the data from one format to another: for example, changing voltage levels and changing analogue data to digital data.

ONLINE TEST

Visit www.brightredbooks.net/N5Computing for a test on computer architecture.

THINGS TO DO AND THINK ABOUT

All computer systems have the same basic structure. They have a processor, memory and buses which work together to execute programs. They also have input, output and storage devices to enter, display and permanently store data. The next time you are sitting at a computer, try to list the input, output and storage devices being used.

OUTCOMES AND UNIT ASSESSMENT

INTRODUCTION

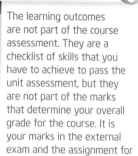

Each of the two mandatory units (Software Design and Development, Information System Design and Development) requires you to achieve an assessment standard in a set of learning outcomes.

In the Software Design and Development unit, there are three learning outcomes.

These are listed below.

ONLINE

You can find more information on the unit assessments for National 5 courses from the Scottish Qualifications Authority at www.brightredbooks.net/ N5Computing

DON'T FORGET

The learning outcomes are not part of the course assessment. They are a checklist of skills that you have to achieve to pass the unit assessment, but they are not part of the marks that determine your overall grade for the course. It is your marks in the external exam and the assignment for the course assessment that determine your grade.

OUTCOMES

Outcome 1

Explain how programs work, drawing on understanding of concepts in software development and basic computer architecture.

Outcome 2

Develop short programs using one or more software-development environments.

Outcome 3

Produce a short, detailed report comparing two contemporary software-development languages or environments.

DETAILS OF THE OUTCOMES

Each of the three learning outcomes has several parts. All of the subsections must be achieved to gain a pass for the outcome.

Outcome 1

This is a written outcome in which you have to show an understanding of how a program works by explaining parts of its code.

There are four subsections to this outcome:

1.1 Reading and explaining code

1.2 Describing the purpose of a range of programming constructs and how they work

1.3 Describing the purpose and role of variables

1.4 Describing how programs relate to low-level operations and structures.

You are expected to be able to explain the purpose of expressions, sequence, selection, iteration and pre-defined functions.

DON'T FORGET

Not all schools will assess this outcome in exactly the same way. You might be given a program listing and be asked to explain the purpose of parts of the code or be asked to explain the effect on the program of changing parts of the code. Some schools might ask for an oral explanation and not require you to give a written answer. So, ask your teacher what you are expected to do to achieve this outcome.

contd

Outcome 2

This is a practical outcome in which you have to develop a series of short programs to implement a range of programming constructs. You also have to test your solutions and correct any errors.

There are five subsections to this outcome:

2.1 Selecting and using a combination of expressions, sequence, selection, iteration and pre-defined functions

2.2 Selecting and using appropriate simple data types, such as numeric (integer and real), string and Boolean

2.3 Testing digital solutions using your own test data

2.4 Identifying and rectifying errors in programs

2.5 Providing internal commentary or documentation.

Your programs should include a minimum of two programming constructs and a minimum of two data types.

Outcome 3

This is an outcome in which you have to produce a report which compares two programming languages.

There are four subsections to this outcome:

3.1 Describing how each language represents standard constructs

3.2 Comparing the range of data types provided in each language

3.3 Comparing the editing features of each language

3.4 Describing how high-level code is translated and executed.

Your report does not need to be a word-processed document. You could use a presentation package, or you could produce a small website to communicate your findings for the report. Your report is not expected to be a very lengthy and time-consuming task. The amount of content would typically equate to about a page or so of text in a word-processing document. You are certainly not expected to write a 10-page document. Of course, you want to do this exercise well, so be concise and highlight your key points, remembering that in report-writing sometimes less is more!

ONLINE

If you decide to use a presentation for your report, you could think about using the online presentation package called Prezi. Prezi is a presentation tool like PowerPoint, but it can be used to zoom in and out of elements of the slides and have a more dynamic effect. It can be learned quite quickly, and there are online tutorials to teach you the basics. Prezi can be found by following the link at www.brightredbooks.net/N5Computing

THINGS TO DO AND THINK ABOUT

The two languages that you compare will depend on your school. You will probably have a main language that you use frequently in your programming lessons, but you should also have been given some experience of another language during the course. If you need more information, don't forget that there are plenty of Internet sites where you can do some research.

SOFTWARE DESIGN AND DEVELOPMENT

QUESTIONS AND ANSWERS 1

DON'T FORGET

Remember that there are questions in the Bright Red Digital Zone which you can use for extra revision.

These questions are intended to be similar to the level and style of questions that you can expect in the exam.

QUESTION 1

(a) Wendy is a student in an architecture college. She uses a CD with a storage capacity of 780 Mb to back up her data. How many CDs would be needed to store the same amount of data as a 16 GB USB memory stick?

(b) Wendy enters the number –87 into a program.

Show how the decimal number –87 is represented in the computer using 8-bit two's complement.

(c) Wendy is filling in a form for a job application on a computer and enters her street address as 1 Beachfront Avenue.

Explain how the computer stores the text for the address.

(d) A logo for a clothes shop was created using a graphics software package.

The blue rectangle is to be made larger. Explain why it is easier to do the editing in a vector graphics package than in a bit-mapped graphics package.

Marks 2, 2, 2, 2

QUESTION 2

Gregg is using a programming language which uses two representations to store floating-point numbers.

Notation A   16-bit exponent   16-bit mantissa
Notation B   8-bit exponent   24-bit mantissa

(a) Describe the terms 'mantissa' and 'exponent'.

(b) Gregg needs to store the floating-point numbers accurately in his program.

State which notation he should choose, and justify your answer.

(c) What would be the effect on the floating-point numbers that are stored in Notation A if the exponent was stored in 24 bits?

Marks 2, 2, 1

QUESTION 3

Sam is writing a book of fairy stories for an e-book which can display the text in seven different languages.

(a) Explain how ASCII code is used to store the following piece of text in binary.

Once upon a time ...

(b) Explain why Unicode should be used to store the text and not ASCII code.

(c) What name is given to non-printing characters such as RETURN and TAB?

(d) How many bytes of storage would be required to store the following sentence in Unicode?

After all, tomorrow is another day.

Marks 1, 1, 1, 2

QUESTION 4

Rosie uses a computer to design posters for a marketing company.

(a) Rosie has just produced a poster but is concerned that the file has a very high capacity.

Describe **two** ways in which Rosie can reduce the file size.

(b) Why do bit-mapped graphics files usually have a higher capacity than vector graphics files?

(c) The image shown alongside was enlarged in a graphics package. State whether bit-mapped or vector graphics were used to create the image, and justify your answer.

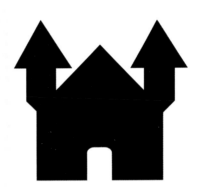 

Marks 2, 2, 2

ANSWER TO QUESTION 1

(a) 16 gigabytes = 16 × 1,024 megabytes = 16,384 megabytes.

The number of CDs = 16,384 / 780 = 21.

(b) The table shows how to find the two's complement of −87.

−128	64	32	16	8	4	2	1	
0	1	0	1	0	1	1	1	87
1	0	1	0	1	0	0	0	Flip 1s and 0s
							+	Add 1
1	0	1	0	1	0	0	1	− 87

(c) The computer stores each character in a unique binary code. A standard is ASCII, which represents each character in an 8-bit code.

(d) A vector graphics package stores the rectangle as an object which can be easily selected and resized. If it was a bit-mapped package, then the rectangle would have to be erased and then redrawn.

ANSWER TO QUESTION 2

(a) The mantissa is the fractional part of a floating-point number that stores the significant figures of the number:

The exponent is the power part of the number.

For example, 101101101011010$= 0.101101011 \times 2^{17}$

↑ ↑
Mantissa Exponent

(b) Gregg should choose Notation B, since it is more accurate because it uses more bits to store the mantissa, which gives more significant figures and hence more accuracy.

(c) Notation A would be able to store a larger range of numbers, since the power can be made higher.

ANSWER TO QUESTION 3

(a) Each character is stored in an 8-bit binary code (including the spaces).

(b) Unicode can store 65,536 characters including the foreign-language characters, whereas the ASCII code system can only store 256 different characters.

(c) These are examples of control characters.

(d) Each character requires 2 bytes of storage.
The sentence requires 70 bytes (28 letters, 5 spaces, a comma and a full stop) of storage.

ANSWER TO QUESTION 4

(a) Reduce the resolution of the image.
Reduce the bit depth of the image.
Use file compression to reduce the file size.

(b) Bit-mapped graphics files are high-capacity because they need to store the colour code of thousands if not millions of pixels.
Vector graphics do not store pixels but just a list of objects with their attributes.

(c) It was created with a bit-mapped graphics package.
The colour codes for the pixels are stored, and so the pixels become jagged and chunky when enlarged.
This would not happen in a vector graphics package because only the attributes of the objects would change, and the size of the pixels is not a factor.

QUESTIONS AND ANSWERS 2

QUESTION 1

A program enters the name, age and height of an applicant for a pilot training course. It then displays a message saying whether the candidate is successful or not.

To be successful, a candidate must be between 18 and 26 years old inclusive and less than 1·8 metres tall.

Part of the program is shown below. The program contains two errors.

```
SET Suitable TO TRUE
RECEIVE Name FROM KEYBOARD
RECEIVE Age FROM KEYBOARD
IF Age < 18 AND Age > 26 THEN SET Suitable TO FALSE
RECEIVE Height FROM KEYBOARD
IF Height < 1·8 THEN SET Suitable TO FALSE
IF Suitable = TRUE THEN
    SEND ["Welcome to the pilot training course."] TO DISPLAY
ELSE
    SEND ["You are not suitable for the pilot training course."] TO DISPLAY
END IF
```

(a) State a suitable data type for the variables Name, Age, Height and Suitable.

(b) Explain why you chose each data type.

(c) There is a mistake in the two instructions shown below.

IF Age < 18 AND Age > 26 THEN SET Suitable TO FALSE

IF Height < 1·8 THEN SET Suitable TO FALSE

Explain the error in each instruction, and write down the corrected instruction.

Marks 4, 4, 4

QUESTION 2

Rewrite both of the following instructions more efficiently by using a different arithmetic operator.

(a) The following instruction is used to treble the score of a player in a game.

SET Score TO Score + Score + Score

(b) The following instruction is used to find the volume of a cube.

SET CubeVolume TO Length * Length * Length

Marks 1, 1

QUESTION 3

A program stores the names of 60 zoo animals in an array. The program declares the array as shown below.

```
DIM Animals(59) As STRING
```

Show how an array could be declared to store each of the following data.

(a) The distances in metres for 20 athletes in a long-jump final.

contd

(b) The names of 10 famous people in Scotland.

(c) The answers to a multiple-choice quiz which has 25 True or False answers.

(d) The seven numbers that are drawn in a National Lottery draw.

Marks 1, 1, 1, 1

QUESTION 4

In a game, a player throws two dice and wins a bonus point if a total score of more than 6 is scored, otherwise a bonus point is deducted. Pseudocode representing part of the program code is shown alongside.

```
SET Total TO Die1 + Die2
IF Total > 6 THEN
    SET Bonus TO Bonus + 1
ELSE
    SET Bonus TO Bonus - 1
END IF
```

(a) The rules of the game are to be changed so that a bonus point is awarded for a total score between 8 and 11 inclusive, otherwise a bonus point is deducted.

Write down a complex condition that would update the program to work correctly for the new rules.

(b) A program enters a temperature and then displays a message saying whether it is freezing or not. (Freezing is zero degrees or below.)

Which of the following conditions are correct?

A   IF Temperature > 0 THEN SEND ["It's freezing!"] TO DISPLAY

B   IF NOT (Temperature > 0) THEN SEND ["It's freezing!"] TO DISPLAY

C   IF Temperature <= 0 THEN SEND ["It's freezing!"] TO DISPLAY

D   IF NOT (Temperature <= 0) SEND ["Its freezing!"] TO DISPLAY

Marks 2, 2

ANSWER TO QUESTION 1

(a) Name should be a STRING data type.

Age should be an INTEGER data type.

Height should be a REAL data type.

Suitable should be a BOOLEAN data type.

(b) The Name variable is storing a piece of text.

The Age variable is storing a whole number, such as 21, 16, 27 and so on.

The Height variable is storing a number which can be a decimal fraction, such as 1·83, 1·69 and so on.

The Suitable variable is storing either True or False.

(c) The condition IF Age < 18 AND Age > 26 can never be true since Age can't be both less than 18 and more than 26 at the same time. The AND should be replaced with an OR so that, if the candidate is under 18 or over 26, then he/she is not suitable.

The correct instruction should be:

IF Age < 18 OR Age > 26 THEN SET Suitable TO FALSE

The candidate is not suitable if he/she is 1·8 m tall or more

The condition IF Height < 1·8 THEN SET Suitable TO FALSE states that a Height of less than 1·8 is unsuitable.

The correct instruction should be:

IF Height >= 1·8 THEN SET Suitable TO FALSE

ANSWER TO QUESTION 2

(a) The addition operator should be replaced by a multiplication operator.

SET Score TO 3 * Score

(b) The multiplication operator should be replaced by a power operator.

SET CubeVolume TO Length ^ 3

ANSWER TO QUESTION 3

(a) DIM Distances(19) As REAL

(b) DIM People(9) As STRING

(c) DIM Answers(24) As BOOLEAN

(d) DIM Animals(6) As INTEGER

ANSWER TO QUESTION 4

(a) IF Total > 7 AND Total < 12 THEN

There are other correct answers which use the 'greater than or equal to' symbols or the 'less than or equal to' symbols.

IF Total >= 8 AND Total <= 11 THEN

IF Total > 7 AND Total <= 11 THEN

IF Total >= 8 AND Total < 12 THEN

(b) A   False

B   True

C   True

D   False

QUESTIONS AND ANSWERS 3

QUESTION 1

Sophie is writing a program that will be used to teach children simple mathematics.

Her program uses fixed and conditional loops to repeat instructions.

(a) Which type of loop is being used in each section of code shown below?

Code A
```
FOR Number FROM 1 TO 12 DO
    SEND [Number * 7] TO DISPLAY
END FOR
```

Code B
```
SET Number TO 0
REPEAT
    SET Number TO Number + 1
    SEND [Number ^ 2] TO DISPLAY
UNTIL Number ^ 2 = 100
```

(b) Explain the difference between these two types of loops.

(c) A program enters the age of a school pupil which must be a number in the range 5 to 18. State which type of loop is used to validate the input.

Marks 2, 2, 1

QUESTION 2

Harry writes computer programs for an insurance company. He uses a lot of pre-defined functions when writing his programs.

(a) Describe two advantages to Harry of using pre-defined functions.

(b) The Mid function returns piece of text from a string variable by specifying the string, a starting position and the number of characters to select.

Study the first two examples and then write down the text returned by the third Mid function.

Example 1   Mid ("Holidays", 5, 3)   Returns the text "day".

Example 2   Mid ("Balance", 2, 4)   Returns the text "alan".

Example 3   Mid ("Mississippi", 7, 3)   ?

Marks 2, 2

QUESTION 3

(a) Examine the following pseudocode:

```
1   SET total TO 0
2   SET count TO 0
3   WHILE count < 5 DO
4       RECEIVE nextinput FROM KEYBOARD
5       SET total TO total + nextinput
6       SET count TO count + 1
7   END WHILE
8   SEND [total / 5] TO DISPLAY
```

Explain the purpose of the pseudocode.

contd

(b) A program simulates a game of dice between two players. In a round, each player rolls two dice and accumulates a total for the points scored on the two dice. The first player to gain a lead of 13 points or more after a round is declared the winner.

Produce pseudocode to solve this problem by putting the following steps into the correct order.

IF TotalA - TotalB > 12 THEN

SEND ["A Won!"] TO DISPLAY

SET ThrowB TO RANDOM 0...12

ELSE

UNTIL TotalA - TotalB > 12 OR TotalB - TotalA > 12

SET TotalA TO TotalA + ThrowA

SET TotalB to 0

REPEAT   END IF   SEND ["B Won!"] TO DISPLAY

SET ThrowA TO RANDOM 0...12

SET TotalA to 0

SET TotalB TO TotalB + ThrowB

Marks 3, 5

QUESTION 4

A program enters the names and heights of two sisters. The program then calculates and displays the name of the taller sister.

Illustrate a solution to this problem in a structure chart.

Marks 4

ANSWER TO QUESTION 4

The following structure diagram solves the problem.

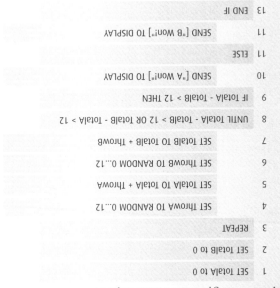

ANSWER TO QUESTION 3

(a) The code enters five numbers from the keyboard and calculates and displays the average of the numbers.

(b) The following pseudocode solves the problem.

1	SET TotalA to 0
2	SET TotalB to 0
3	REPEAT
4	SET ThrowA TO RANDOM 0...12
5	SET TotalA TO TotalA + ThrowA
6	SET ThrowB TO RANDOM 0...12
7	SET TotalB TO TotalB + ThrowB
8	UNTIL TotalA - TotalB > 12 OR TotalB - TotalA > 12
9	IF TotalA - TotalB > 12 THEN
10	SEND ["A Won!"] TO DISPLAY
11	ELSE
11	SEND ["B Won!"] TO DISPLAY
13	END IF

ANSWER TO QUESTION 2

(a) The programmer saves time because he/she does not have to write the instructions from scratch.

Also, the function is tried and tested and will be free of errors, which might not be the case if written by the programmer.

(b) Mid ("Mississippi", 7, 3) returns the text "sip".

ANSWER TO QUESTION 1

(a) Code A is using a fixed loop.

Code B is using a conditional loop.

(b) A conditional loop repeats a group of instructions until a condition is true.

A fixed loop repeats a group of instructions a pre-determined number of times.

(c) Validation requires a conditional loop.

QUESTIONS AND ANSWERS 4

QUESTION 1

Programs are tested to locate and remove any errors.

(a) Errors can be classified as syntax, execution or logic errors.

Describe each of these three types of error.

(b) Which type of error is present in each of the following pieces of programming code?

A	Let Area = Length + Breadth
B	Let MyShare = PrizeMoney / 0
C	Let NetSalary = Tax – GrossSalary
D	Let Average = Score1 + Score2 / 2
E	Ify Age > 21 Then Suitable = False

Marks 3, 5

QUESTION 2

A programmer is writing part of a program which enters the number of living grandparents a child has. The number is validated to be in the range 0 to 4.

The programmer tests the code by entering '3', which is accepted by the program. The programmer then concludes that the programming is correct.

(a) Explain why the programmer cannot be sure that the program is correct without further testing.

(b) Supply two other sets of test data that would test the program more fully, and give a reason why you chose each set of data.

Marks 2, 2

QUESTION 3

A program enters the age of a man and the age of his dog.

The program then calculates and displays the age of the dog in human years and also displays the age of the man.

The program then displays a message saying whether the man is older, the dog is older or they are both the same age in human years.

(1 dog year equals 7 human years.)

(a) Write down three sets of test data that could be used to thoroughly test the program, and give a reason why you chose each set of test data.

(b) What output should each set of test data display?

Marks 6, 3

QUESTION 4

A program enters the name of an animal and its life expectancy in years.

The life expectancy is validated to be in the range 1 to 150.

The program then displays a message stating whether the animal has a short, medium or long life expectancy. (Short = under 20 years, Medium = 20 to 60 years,
Long = over 60 years.)

Pseudocode illustrating the design of the program logic is shown below.

Suggest how meaningful identifiers and indentation can be used to make the program design more readable.

```
RECEIVE a FROM KEYBOARD
REPEAT
RECEIVE b FROM KEYBOARD
IF b < 1 OR b > 150 THEN
SEND ["That can't be the right life expectancy!"] TO DISPLAY
END IF
UNTIL b > 0 AND b < 151
IF b < 20 THEN
SEND [a, " has a short life expectancy."] TO DISPLAY
END IF
IF b >= 20 AND b <= 60 Then
SEND [a, " has a medium life expectancy."] TO DISPLAY
END IF
IF b > 60 THEN
SEND [a, " has a long life expectancy."] TO DISPLAY
END IF
```

Marks 2

ANSWER TO QUESTION 1

(a) Syntax errors are errors which break the rules of the language, such as misspelling a command word.

Execution errors are errors detected during the running of the program, such as dividing by zero, which is not possible mathematically.

Logic errors are errors in the logic of the code itself, such as subtracting two numbers the wrong way round.

(b) A Logic error, since Area should be Length times Breadth.

B Execution error, since you can't divide by zero.

C Logic error, since NetSalary should be GrossSalary – Tax.

D Logic error, since Average should be (Score1 – Score2) / 2.

E Syntax error, since If has been misspelt as Ify.

ANSWER TO QUESTION 2

(a) Just because the program works for 3 grandparents does not mean that it will work for all possible cases. The program should be tested with extreme numbers which lie on the boundaries, or with exceptional data.

(b) Test data 1
Grandparents = 4
This is to test whether the program works on the extremities of valid data. (Grandparents = 0 could be chosen for the same reason.)

Test data 2
Grandparents = 7
This is to test whether the program works with exceptional data that is outwith the possible values. (Other examples of exceptional data could be Grandparents = –3, Grandparents = Ted, etc.)

ANSWER TO QUESTION 3

(a) Test data 1
Dog age = 3, Human age = 15
This data is chosen to test the situation where the dog is older than the man in human years.

Test data 2
Dog age = 7, Human age = 60
This data is chosen to test the situation where the man is older than the dog in human years.

Test data 3
Dog age = 5, Human age = 35
This data is chosen to test the situation where the dog and the man are the same age in human years.

(b) Test 1 output
Dog's human age 21, Man's age 15. The dog is older.

Test 2 output
Dog's human age 49, Man's age 60. The man is older.

Test 3 output
Dog's human age 35, Man's age 35. They are the same age.

ANSWER TO QUESTION 4

The variable names can be changed into meaningful identifiers such as Animal_Name and Life_Expectancy instead of a and b.

The Ifs and the REPEAT ... UNTIL ... loop can be indented to make the instructions stand out more.

QUESTIONS AND ANSWERS 5

QUESTION 1

High-level languages require a compiler or an interpreter to translate the program.

(a) Which of the following statements are true about interpreters and compilers?

    A Interpreted programs run faster than compiled programs.

    B A compiled program uses up less memory than an interpreted program.

    C They both produce object code.

    D It is easier to correct errors in an interpreted program than in a compiled program.

    E They both translate high-level languages into machine code.

    F Both an interpreted and a compiled program are translated before they are executed.

(b) The computer programmer in an astrology department in a university has written software to process data collected from their telescopes. After 6 months, the astronomers realise that there are errors in the program. The programmer has a copy of the program's object code but not the source code.

    (i) Which type of translator was used to produce this program?

    (ii) Can the program be changed to correct the errors? Explain your answer.

Marks 6, 2

QUESTION 2

At one time, all computer programs were written in machine code. Nowadays, almost all software is written in a high-level language.

(a) Why is it difficult and time-consuming to write programs in machine code?

(b) Give two features of high-level languages.

(c) At one time, documents were produced in offices by secretaries using typewriters.

    Computer programs such as word-processors and databases are now used in offices to create and organise data.

    Give one environmental impact resulting from the introduction of computer programs in offices.

Marks 2, 2, 1

QUESTION 3

Shown below is a diagram of a computer system.

DON'T FORGET

It is a common fault to answer your own question instead of the exam question.
Read the preamble for the question carefully and be sure that you are answering the requirements of the questions. For example, if asked to compare two processes, don't just give a description of each process.

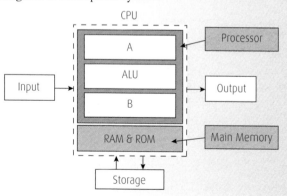

contd

(a) What function does the ALU perform apart from arithmetic calculations?

(b) Name the two other components of the processor, A and B.

(c) Main memory is made up of two types, RAM and ROM. A data file is loaded into main memory to be edited.

State whether the data file is stored in RAM or ROM, and explain your answer.

(d) The processor has three buses to connect it with main memory.

Describe the functions, of the three buses.

Marks 1, 2, 2, 3

QUESTION 4

A laser printer is attached to a desktop computer. An interface between the processor and printer provides a physical link and compensates for differences in how they operate. Two functions of the interface are data storage and data conversion.

Explain why the interface needs to perform data storage and data conversion.

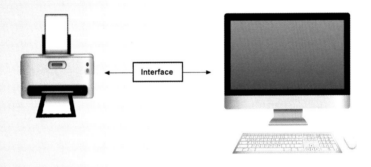

Interface

Marks 2

ANSWER TO QUESTION 1

(a) A False B True C False D True E True F False

(b) (i) A compiler was used because it produces object code, which is not the case with an interpreter.

(ii) The program cannot be edited, because it requires the source code to be edited.

Only the object code is available, which is in machine code, and it would be extremely difficult to edit a machine-code program.

ANSWER TO QUESTION 2

(a) Machine-code instructions are in binary code, so it is very easy to make mistakes with the codes; and reading code to make changes and locate errors is fraught with difficulty. Also, a single machine-code instruction does very little processing, and it takes many instructions to perform the same amount of processing as one instruction in a high-level language.

(b) Any two of the following features are good answers.

High-level languages use English for command words.
Complex arithmetic can be performed in one instruction.
They have inbuilt functions.
One high-level instruction translates into many machine-code instructions.
The program can be broken down into procedures.

(c) Saves paper by storing data electronically.

Saves space and the need for filing cabinets.

There are dangers from the disposal of computing equipment, which contains toxic materials.

There are fewer jobs, since people can be more productive at a computer.

ANSWER TO QUESTION 3

(a) The ALU performs logical decisions (AND, OR, NOT) as well as calculations.

(b) The other two components are the control unit and registers.

(c) The data file is loaded into RAM (Random-Access Memory) RAM can be written to, but ROM can only be read from and not written to.

(d) The address bus specifies which memory location to read data from or write data to.

The control bus sends out signals to initiate events such as reading or writing data.

The data bus is used to carry data from a memory location to the processor and vice versa.

ANSWER TO QUESTION 4

A printer operates at a much slower speed than the processor. Therefore the interface needs to temporarily store data sent from the processor until the printer is ready to accept it.

Data conversion is required to change the format of the data stored on the processor to the format in which it is stored on the printer. For example, voltage levels may need to be converted.

INFORMATION SYSTEM DESIGN AND DEVELOPMENT

DATABASE STRUCTURE 1

VIDEO

Watch the clip about databases at www.brightredbooks.net/N5Computing

WHAT IS A DATABASE?

A **database** is an organised collection of records holding data so that it can be stored and accessed quickly. Before computers, organisations such as banks, schools and supermarkets kept their data on a large number of paper records in filing cabinets. The advantages of keeping data on a computer include speed of retrieval of information, easier amendments to data, less waste of paper and space, and password protection to improve the security of files.

FIELDS, RECORDS AND FILES

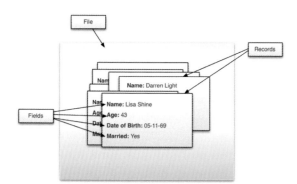

File

A database **file** is an organised collection of records on a particular topic. For example, a sports club may keep a file on its members' details, or a zoo may keep a file on the details of each of their animals.

Record

A **record** is the data held on one person or thing: for example, a student record in a school database, or an article record in a supermarket stock file.

Field

A **field** is the term given to one item of data in a record: for example, the age field in an employee's record, or the price field in a stock record.

SEARCHING AND SORTING

Selection

Records in a database can be selected according to certain rules based on one or more fields. For example, **searching** a student database for male students who are over 15 years old can be achieved by selecting records where the Sex field = 'Male' and the Age field > 15.

Sorting

Sorting a database means to arrange the records in order. The records can be put in ascending or descending order of one or more fields.

Shown below is a database that has been sorted on two fields. The records have been sorted primarily on the Sex field in ascending order and then on the Age field in descending order.

Sex	Age	Street	City
F	24	2 North St.	Glasgow
F	21	66 Brook St.	Glasgow
F	20	23 Hamilton Cres.	Edinburgh
F	20	10 High St.	Glasgow
F	19	125 Laurel Av.	London
F	19	20 Black St.	Glasgow
M	22	666 Swan St.	Motherwell
M	20	99 Cone Cres.	Helensburgh
M	19	33 Perth Rd.	Glasgow
M	17	4 Cruise Dr.	Dundee
......	......	......	......

FIELD TYPES

Text

A **text field** stores a string of characters.
Examples of a text field are Surname, Town, Colour and so on.

Numbers

A **numeric field** stores numbers.
Examples of a numeric field are Age, Height, Population and so on.

Date

A **date field** stores a date.
Examples of a date field are Date of Birth, Return to School Date, M.O.T. Date and so on.

Time

A **time field** stores a time of day.
Examples of a time field are Start Time, Appointment Time, Closing Time and so on.

Graphics

A **graphics field** stores an image.
Examples of a graphics field are Student Photo, Company Logo, Country Flag and so on.

Calculation

A **calculation field** (sometimes called a computed field) is calculated from a formula which uses other fields in the record.
For example, an Average field could be calculated from three other fields called Test 1, Test 2 and Test 3 using the formula = ([Test 1] + [Test 2] + [Test 3]) / 3

Link

A **link field** stores a **hyperlink** within the database file or a hyperlink to a document outside the database file.
The link could be to a specific record in the database file, another relevant document, an Internet site and so on.

Boolean

A **Boolean field** stores just two values, Yes and No.
Examples of a Boolean field are Subscription Paid, Book Returned, Married and so on.

Key Field

A **key field** stores a value that is unique to each record so that it can be specifically identified.
Examples of a key field are Reference Number, Student Number, Account Number and so on.

 DON'T FORGET

The fields in a database can store different types of information. Some will contain numbers, others will store text, some will be holding a date and so on. Databases allow the designer of the database to specify the field type of each field so that the data can be stored and processed in a particular way.

 DON'T FORGET

A time field stores a time of day in hours, minutes and seconds, and not the time taken for something to take place. For example, the time taken for an athlete to run the 100 metres would be stored in a numeric field and not a time field.

 ONLINE TEST

Test yourself on database structures online at www.brightredbooks.net/N5Computing

 THINGS TO DO AND THINK ABOUT

Creating a database involves the design of the structure of the records. This involves creating the necessary fields to hold the data and specifying their field types.

The design of the database will have consequences for how the data can be retrieved and sorted.

DATABASE STRUCTURE 2

VALIDATION OF DATA

There are various aspects of ensuring that data entered by the user is valid and acceptable.

A **field-length check** forces the data which is entered to be a specified number of characters long. For example, a code for an item in a catalogue may be required to be 8 characters long. If the user does not enter the required number of characters, then he/she is given an error message and asked to try again.

A **range check** forces the data which is entered to lie in a certain range of values. For example, a mark in an exam out of 50 must be entered as a number between 0 and 50; or a month entered as a number will only accept values from 1 to 12.

Restricted choice

A restricted choice forces the data which is entered to lie within a list of acceptable value. For example a day of the week must be entered as Monday, Tuesday, Wednesday, Thursday, Friday, Saturday or Sunday.

Presence check

Checks that important data has not been missed out and is actually present.

For example, customers may be required to enter their postcode.

FLAT FILE AND RELATIONAL DATABASES

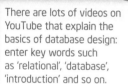

VIDEO

There are lots of videos on YouTube that explain the basics of database design: enter key words such as 'relational', 'database', 'introduction' and so on.

A **flat-file database** contains records in only one table of data. This is fine for a simple situation such as storing the records of pupils in a school, where the only requirements of the database are to store their personal details and to access records quickly.

Most companies need to store data in a much more complex way than that performed by a single-table flat-file database. They use a **relational database**, which allows data to be stored in several linked tables. For example, a relational database used in business may store a table for employee records, customer records, product records, order records and so on. These tables are linked together to reduce the duplication of data and to allow the automatic update of details in tables when the data in a linked table is changed.

For example, if the data was stored in one table in a flat file, then every order record would require all of the fields associated with the customer, the employee who placed the order, and the product, to be stored in the record. In a relational database, the order record only requires one field to link to the details in each of the other tables and so removes the duplication of data.

LINKED TABLES

Key Field

A **key field** is a field in a record that is used to uniquely identify a record in the database. Using a name or date of birth as the key field is not a good idea because, in a large database with thousands of records, two or more people could easily have the same name or date of birth. Key fields are usually special codes or numbers that store an item of data that is unique to each record. Account number, member code or reference number are common examples of key fields.

Primary Keys and Foreign Keys

A primary key and a **foreign key** are used to make relationships between tables.

A primary key is the field that is used to uniquely identify each record in a table. A table can have only one primary key.

A foreign key contains values that correspond to values in the primary key of another table. For example, in a Flights table for an airport database, each Flight record has a Pilot ID field that corresponds to a record in a Pilots table. The Pilot ID field is a primary key of the Pilot table and a foreign key of the Flights table. When a record is added to the Flights table, a value for the Pilot ID comes from the Pilots table.

This means that all of the fields for the pilot are not stored in each Flight record but are simply a foreign key that links to the fields in the Pilot table.

The diagram below illustrates the relationship between the tables.

The small pictures of a key indicate the primary key in each table.

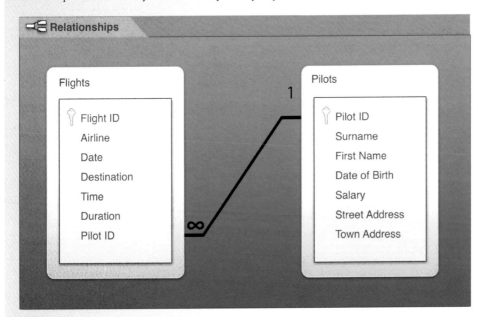

DON'T FORGET

A one-to-many relationship between tables is illustrated by using the symbols 1 and ∞. The ∞ symbol is used in mathematics to represent infinity, but in relational databases it represents many.

This is an example of a one-to-many relationship. This means that one Pilot ID from the Pilots table will appear in many records in the Flights table. This is a common type of relationship: one product ID will appear in many order records, one author ID will appear in many book records and so on.

ONLINE TEST

Test yourself on database structures online at www. brightredbooks.net/ N5Computing

 THINGS TO DO AND THINK ABOUT

As part of your practical work for this course, you will be required to create a relational database structure to store information. Use the theory work covered in the database section of this book as an aid to help you understand the principles involved in database design for this task.

WEBSITES

INTRODUCTION

The **World Wide Web** (WWW) consists of multimedia information stored on the Internet on websites.

The websites are made up of pages which consist of the multimedia elements text, graphics, video and sound. Other elements such as navigation tabs, tables, hyperlinks and so on are commonly used.

At one time, websites were created using **Hypertext Mark-up Language** (HTML), but this was very difficult and time-consuming, and these days most websites are created using a web-page editor. Web-page editors allow elements of the website to be dragged and dropped onto the page without the need for writing technically difficult HTML code to achieve the same thing.

BROWSER

A **browser** is a program that displays web pages and allows the user to navigate around other websites on the Internet. Internet Explorer is the most commonly used browser.

Browsers provide other functions such as:

1 Allowing the user to keep a list of shortcuts to favourite websites so that they can quickly be revisited.
2 Keeping a history of recently visited websites.
3 Accessing webmail to send and receive e-mails.
4 The settings can be customised to suit the preferences of the user, for example controlling which toolbars are displayed, which website is initially displayed, the zoom-in/zoom-out factor and so on.
5 Performing the transfer of files over the Internet using the File Transfer Protocol (FTP).

HYPERLINK

DON'T FORGET

An external hyperlink is a link to a different website, whereas an internal hyperlink is a link to another page or file within the same website.

A **hyperlink** is usually a piece of coloured text or an image which, when clicked, provides a connection to another page within the site or to another website. Hyperlinks allow the user to navigate within a site or to find further information in other websites.

Absolute hyperlink. An absolute hyperlink refers to the use of the complete URL. Example: http://wvvw.bbc.co.uk/weather.html

Relative hyperlink. A relative hyperlink uses a path from the current page to the destination page. Example: /sport.html

contd

Hotspots

A **hotspot** is an active area of the screen which triggers an event when the mouse pointer is hovered over it. The mouse-pointer icon usually changes to represent the context of the event.

For example, a birthday website may include a screen showing presents and items of food. When the mouse pointer is hovered over one of these items, the icon changes to a musical note, and a suitable song is played.

A hotspot is not the same as a hyperlink. A hyperlink requires the user to click on text or an image, but a hotspot only requires the user to hover over the 'hot' area of the screen.

URL

Websites can be visited by entering a unique address called a **Uniform Resource Locator** (URL) into a browser program. The URL is made up of several component parts. These parts include the protocol, the domain name, the path to the file and the name of the file.

For example, the URL for a web page about laptops made by Dell on the PC World website is shown below.

http://www.pcworld.co.uk/hardware/laptops/dell.htm

Protocol   Domain name   Pathway   Filename

The **protocol** is an agreed set of rules between the sender and the receiver that is used to transfer the file. In this case, the Hypertext Transfer Protocol (HTTP) is used to transfer a web page.

The **domain name** is the address of the server computer that is hosting the web page. Dots are used to separate the different parts (two or more) of the domain name. The pars are used to specify the type of organisation and the country in which it is based.

The tables alongside show some examples of the parts used in domain names for commonly used organisations and countries.

The pathway specifies the route to the page.

The filename is the name of the actual file that is being accessed.

If the URL is not known for a particular website, then the site and other relevant sites can be found by entering suitable keywords into a **search engine**.

NAVIGATION

Browsers provide several ways to allow the user to move between different websites and web pages. Specific sites can be found by entering the URL into the browser, or a search engine can be used to find sites on a certain topic by entering appropriate keywords. Backward and forward arrows can also be used to move back and forth to revisit sites and then move forwards to more recently viewed sites. Websites that are frequently visited can be saved as favourite shortcuts so that they can be accessed quickly without the need for entering the URL.

Most websites also contain a tab control that allows the user to go directly to any page in the site at any time with one click of the mouse.

THINGS TO DO AND THINK ABOUT

Websites are made up of pages of multimedia content. They can be found using a URL or a search engine or by following hyperlinks between different sites.

ONLINE

Go online and download some of the websites that are stored in your favourites. Investigate the component parts of the URL displayed at the top of the screen in the browser.

Part	Meaning
.com	A company
.edu	An educational institution
.org	A non-profit-making institution
.gov	A governmental agency

Part	Country
.uk	United Kingdom
.fr	France
.nz	New Zealand
.it	Italy

DON'T FORGET

Universal Resource Locator is another expansion of the acronym URL as well as Uniform Resource Locator, but the phrase Uniform Resource Locator is used in this course.

ONLINE TEST

Test yourself on websites at www.brightredbooks.net/N5Computing

USER INTERFACE

INTRODUCTION

The **user interface** is a term used to describe how the user communicates with a computer program.

Early computers in the 1950s used punched cards to enter programs and data into the computer. If there was an error, then the cards had to be repunched and entered again. It could take weeks to get a program running successfully. In the last 30 years, the user interface has evolved through keyboard input, the mouse, speech recognition and, more recently, touch-sensitive screens. Technologies that allow users to control their computers with body gestures (like Wii or Kinect) are improving and being used more widely. Some people think that, in the future, people may use thoughts to allow brain waves to communicate with a computer.

WIMP (WINDOWS, ICONS, MENUS, POINTER)

Most modern desktop and laptop computers use a graphical interface called **WIMP** or sometimes GUI (Graphical User Interface). In this type of interface, the mouse or some other pointing device is used to select from a list of choices on pull-down menus and small pictures called icons.

The main advantage of this type of system is its ease of use to non-technical users. However, an expert user can find this interface slow and clumsy.

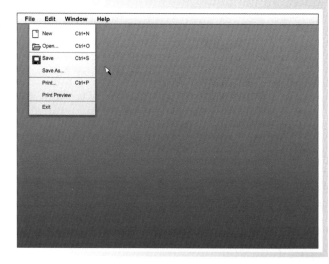

ONLINE

Investigate the history of the development of the user interface at www.brightredbooks.net/N5Computing

USER REQUIREMENTS

Visual Layout

The **visual layout** is rules from photography and painting that govern the appearance of the screen so that it is not too cluttered and is easy to take in.

For example, colour panels can be used to identify different areas of the screen which have a different purpose. Bold and coloured text can be used to highlight an important element of the screen. The 'rule of thirds' can be used, where the screen is divided into horizontal or vertical thirds.

DON'T FORGET

Keyboard shortcuts allow an option to be selected by pressing a special combination of keys (e.g. Control B for bold text). Learning these commands can considerably speed up your work compared to moving the pointer and clicking with the mouse.

Navigation

It is important to make **navigation** around the software package as easy as possible. Backward and forward arrows can be useful as well as the ability to undo an unwanted action. Most software packages allow the undoing of several steps, and some even allow you to go back to the start of the session even if it involves hundreds of steps.

contd

Selection

Selection is how interface controls are used to pick options.

For example, pop-up and drop-down menus are used to select from a restricted list, radio buttons are used for one option to make a compulsory choice, and checkboxes are used to select zero, one or several options.

Consistency

A good user interface will have a **consistent** format for menu choices, fonts and the visual display. This makes it easier to learn the package, since the interaction with the software is always presented in a similar way. Once one part of a package has been learned, it is easier to learn the rest of the package.

Interactivity

Interactivity concerns the controls that determine how the user interacts with the interface. This can be done with buttons, sliders, control bars and text boxes.

Readability

It is important that instructions are **easy to read** and to follow. Commands should be labelled with simple verbs such as Run, Insert, Undo and so on. Too much text can take too long to read and can clutter up the screen.

Warnings and Error Messages

A good user interface will give a **warning** before the user performs a potentially destructive action. For example, if files are about to be deleted, then the user should be asked 'Are you sure?' and be given the chance to abort the action.

Customising the Interface

It is often possible for the user interface to be **customised** to suit the preferences of the individual user.

For example, changes can be made to the contents of menus, the colour scheme and fonts used in menus and dialogue boxes. This can improve the efficiency of the user by making the commands that are used the most frequently readily available.

Accessibility

Accessibility is hardware and software technologies that help physically impaired people to use a computer.

Screen magnification/zoom feature for vision impaired users, voice input/output for users with speech and hearing difficulties, etc. can make computers more accessible to all users.

DON'T FORGET

The age-range of the user will also determine the design of the interface. For example, a very young child who can barely read will be able to click on the icons for the tools in a painting program but would find it impossible to perform the same choices through words displayed in menus.

TYPE OF USER

The age and ability of the **user** have to be considered when designing the user interface. If the computer system is for non-technical users, then a graphical user interface involving pointing with the mouse is the usual preference. With this type of interface, the novice user does not need to remember commands given through the keyboard and can explore pull-down menus and icons to make choices. However, an expert user would prefer to use keyboard shortcuts rather than continually switch between moving the mouse and entering data from the keyboard, which he/she would find inefficient.

ONLINE TEST

Test yourself on user interfaces online at www.brightredbooks.net/N5Computing

THINGS TO DO AND THINK ABOUT

The user interface for mobile phones changes rapidly. Think about how the mobiles that you have owned have changed over the years in their user input and navigation.

TYPES OF MEDIA

TEXT, SOUND, GRAPHICS AND VIDEO

Computers are required to store text, sound, graphics and video data. For example, desktop publishing software uses a combination of text and graphics data, and website design uses a combination of text, graphics, video and sound data. The different types of data can be stored in text, graphics, video and sound files which can be imported directly into documents as required.

STANDARD FILE FORMATS

ONLINE

Use the Internet to research the technical details of different file formats. Enter the acronyms RTF, GIF, MP3 etc. into a search engine together with keywords such as 'technical', 'description', 'details' etc.

A **standard file format** is a file format that is recognised by other computer programs different from the one that was used to create it. This makes it possible to transfer a file to all programs that recognise the standard format.

For example, if a text document is created in Microsoft Word and then saved as a Word file, then it could not be easily opened by another word-processing program. However, if it is saved in a standard file format for text such as RTF, then other programs can recognise and open the file. The disadvantage is that formatting information such as indents and tables can be lost.

Standard file formats exist for text, sound, graphics and video files. Some examples of standard file formats are described below.

Text

TXT stands for text. It is a file format that stores the characters in the document but not any formatting information apart from control characters such as RETURN and TAB.

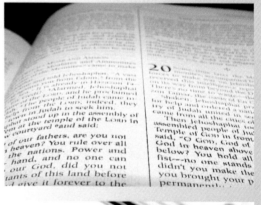

RTF is a file format that contains formatting information including font, font size and styles such as bold and underline as well as which characters are stored.

DON'T FORGET

RTF stands for Rich Text Format, since it is 'richer' than the TXT file format, which is poorer in its formatting information.

Audio

WAV (Waveform Audio Format) is a file format for sound which uses lossless compression.

MP3 stands for layer 3 of the MPEG-1 standard file format. It is a file format that uses lossy compression, so that the quality is reduced. However, techniques such as removing sounds that are inaudible to the human ear can mean that the reduction in quality is barely noticeable. This format is widely used to store music files on computer and portable devices, because typically files are compressed to about one tenth of their size.

contd

Graphics

BMP is shorthand for bitmap. It is a file format that uses a binary code to store the colour of each pixel. This format does not use compression, so that the file sizes can be very large. BMP files can have bit depth of 24 bits, which provides over 16 million colours.

GIF (Graphics Interchange Format) is a file format that uses lossless compression. GIF uses a bit depth of 8 bits, which gives a maximum of 256 colours.

JPEG (Joint Photographic Expert Group) is a file format that uses lossy compression, which means that the quality of the image may be impaired. JPEG uses a bit depth of 24 bits, which provides over 16 million colours.

PNG (Portable Network Graphics) is a file format for graphics that supports over 16 million colours. PNG can provide lossless compression.

Video

Video files are made up of graphics frames that are typically displayed around 20 times per second to create movement. Since video files can be extremely high-capacity, they are normally stored in a compressed file format to reduce their size.

MPEG (Motion Picture Experts Group) is a file format that uses lossy compression.

AVI (Audio Video Interleave) is an uncompressed file format for video.

Spreadsheets

Microsoft Excel spreadsheets have the file extension .XLS

There are other spreadsheets apart from Microsoft Excel. Standard file formats exist so that a document created in one spreadsheet can be opened by other spreadsheets. However, some of the formatting and functions may be lost if they are not supported by the standard file format.

CSV (Comma-Separated Values) is a standard file format that can be used to save tabular data such as spreadsheets by using symbols to separate the rows and columns.

	A	B	C
1	NAME	CLUB	TIME
2	Alan W.	Hares	16.30
3	Rosie H.	Bright Red	16.55
4	Alan G.	Bright Red	17.15
5	Sabrina M.	Irish Rovers	17.19
6	John M.	Bright Red	17.43
7	Norrie G.	SUH	18.12
8	Gavin S.	Forfar Bridies	20.47
9	Richard B.	Wizards of Oz	22.10
10	Caleb R.	Tortoises	25.20

XML (Extensible Mark-up Language)
This is another standard file format that can be used to store spreadsheet files. It is commonly used with HTML documents.

PDF

PDF stands for Portable Document Format. It is a multi-platform file format that captures the text, graphics and formatting of documents from a variety of application programs. It means that documents that are saved in this file format can be opened by different programs on a PC or a Mac and will look the same.

ONLINE TEST

Test how well you know about data types online at www.brightredbooks.net/N5Computing

THINGS TO DO AND THINK ABOUT

Standard file formats exist to make it easier to transfer data between different computer programs. There are several other standard formats available for text, sound, graphics and video files, but the key ones are listed in this book.

FACTORS AFFECTING FILE SIZE

INTRODUCTION

The quality of graphics, video and sound files is determined by factors such as resolution, colour depth and sampling rate. A computer has a limited amount of storage capacity in main memory and backing store. There is always a balance between improving the quality by increasing the resolution, colour depth and sampling rate and the very large file sizes that result. Compression techniques are used to reduce the size of large multimedia files. **Lossless compression** results in no reduction in quality, but **lossy compression** reduces the quality of the file.

FILE SIZE AND QUALITY

There are several factors that affect the quality of graphics, sound and video files. However, improving the quality has the disadvantage of increasing the file size, since more bits need to be used to store the extra details.

Resolution

The term **resolution** is a measure of the size of the pixels in an image.

High-resolution graphics have a large number of small pixels.

Low-resolution graphics have a small number of large pixels.

High-resolution graphics have a better quality than low-resolution graphics but have a larger file size since they have to store the colours of more pixels.

The resolution of graphics is usually measured in d.p.i. (dots per inch).

Colour Depth

Bit-mapped graphics use binary codes to represent the colour of each pixel. **Colour depth** is the number of bits that are used for the colour code of each pixel. The higher the number of bits, then the higher the number of colours that can be represented.

Increasing the colour depth will give better-quality colour graphics with a wider range of colours but will also increase the file size.

Sampling Rate

Digital sound is created by taking a sample of a sound many times every second. The **sampling rate** is the number of times that the sound is sampled per second.

A higher sample rate will result in a better-quality digitised sound but will increase the file size, as more sound samples are stored per second. Sampling rates are of the order of many thousands of times per second.

Frame Rate

The quality of video data is determined by the number of frames that are captured per second. Each frame has settings for resolution and colour depth. The file size increases for higher **frame rates**, resolution and colour depth.

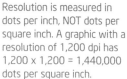

DON'T FORGET

Resolution is measured in dots per inch, NOT dots per square inch. A graphic with a resolution of 1,200 dpi has 1,200 x 1,200 = 1,440,000 dots per square inch.

DON'T FORGET

Don't confuse sampling rate with sample size. Sample size is the number of bits used to store each sound sample. The higher the sample size, then the better the quality of the sound, since the sample represents the sound with higher definition, but the file size will increase. Typically, sample sizes of 8 bits and 16 bits are used.

STORAGE CALCULATIONS

A black-and-white graphic has pixels that can have only two possible states, i.e. black or white. Therefore the colour of each pixel can be stored in 1 bit, with black represented by a 1 and white represented by a 0.

The black-and-white graphic shown below contains $480 \times 360 = 172,800$ pixels.

Each pixel requires 1 bit of storage.

Total storage requirements = 172,800 bits
                      = 172,800 / 8 bytes
                      = 21,600 bytes
                      = 21,600 / 1,024 Kb
                      = 21·1 Kb.

Colour Bitmap Calculation

If the above black and white image (1 bit per pixel) was stored in colour then each pixel would increase by a factor depending on the colour depth (number of bits per pixel).

If the colour depth was 24 bits instead of black and white then the storage requirements would be 24 times higher.

The colour graphic above contains $480 \times 360 = 172,800$ pixels.

Each pixel requires 24 bits of storage.

Total storage requirements = $172,800 \times 24$ bits = $\frac{4,147,200}{8}$ bytes = 518,400 bytes = $\frac{518,400}{1024}$ Kb = 506.25 Kb

NEED FOR COMPRESSION

Graphic, video and sound files can be very large. These files can be **compressed** to reduce their file size, but they must be decompressed before they can be used. There are two main advantages of compressing large files on a computer system.

1 Compressed files require less storage space than uncompressed files on storage devices such as hard discs.

2 Compressed files can be transmitted faster over the Internet or a computer network, since there is a smaller number of bits to be transferred.

 THINGS TO DO AND THINK ABOUT

Look into the settings available for the graphics, video and sound-editing software that you use. Try different settings for resolution, colour depth and so on, and see how they affect the resulting file size.

 DON'T FORGET

File compression can be either lossy or lossless. Lossy compression reduces the file size but at the expense of detail and quality. Lossless compression uses mathematical techniques to reduce the file size with no loss of detail or quality.

 ONLINE

Find out how file compression works at www.brightredbooks.net/ N5Computing

 ONLINE TEST

Test how well you have learned the factors affecting file size at www. brightredbooks.net/ N5Computing

SCRIPTING, MARK-UP LANGUAGES AND TESTING

SCRIPTING LANGUAGES

Application programs such as Microsoft Word and Excel include a **scripting language** that allows the user to customise the package and automate tasks. An expert user can use the scripting language to write code to perform tasks beyond the features offered by the basic package. A non-expert user can use a macro to record a series of mouse clicks and keystrokes which are stored in the scripting language. The macro can then be played back over and over again to save the user time when the same task is required again in the future.

The macro is usually run by attaching it to an icon or a keyboard shortcut.

Shown below is the code for a macro which places the user's name in the document in a font, fontsize and style to make it look like a signature.

```
Sub Macro I ()
'This macro enters my name in a font that looks like a signature
    Selection.Font.Name = "Freestyle Script"
    Selection.Font.Size = 18
    Selection.Font.Italic = wdToggle
    Selection.TypeText Text:="Polly Wiggins"
End Sub
```

MARK-UP LANGUAGES

Hypertext Mark-up Language (HTML) is a language used to create web pages.

HTML consists of a series of short codes called tags which are entered into a text file by the author of the site. The text is then saved as an HTML file which can then be displayed in a browser such as Internet Explorer, Chrome and Firefox. The browser reads the file and translates the text into its visible form in the browser.

Tags

Tags are used to create a description of the web page by identifying elements on the page such as a header, title, body, style, font size, image, hyperlink and so on.

```
<html>
    <head>
        <title> My first web page </title>
    </head>
    <body>
        <h1> Welcome to my first web page! </h1>
        <p> This text is in normal style </p>
        <p> <b> This text is in bold </b></p>
        <p> <u> This text is underlined </u> </p>
        <p align = "center"> This text is centred </p>
    </body>
</html>
```

A tag can be put inside another tag. This is called nested tags.

Alongside is an example of a simple HTML page.

The <html> tags always surround the whole file to specify what type of file it is.

The <head> tags define the head element, which contains some header information such as the title of the page which is contained in the <title> tag.

The <body> tags surround the main content of the file such as text, images and tables.

The <h1> (headline size 1), <p> (new paragraph), <b> (bold) and <u> (underline) tags are used for text formatting.

Hyperlinks can be achieved by specifying a URL and some text to activate the link.

```
<p><a href="http://www.bbc.co.uk//">BBC Website</a></p>
```

JAVASCRIPT

This is a programming language that can be incorporated into HTML pages. It is a scripting language and therefore cannot be used to create stand-alone programs. **JavaScript** is used to add interactivity to web pages and make them more dynamic. For example, JavaScript can be used to validate data that is entered into forms, give warnings and confirmation messages to the user and provide information on the system date and time. Command buttons, check boxes, radio buttons and other controls can be added to web pages to provide added functionality.

The example alongside asks the user to enter their name and then gives a personal welcome followed by a message stating how many days are left until Christmas.

The tags <script type="text/javascript"> and </script> are placed in the <head> section to declare the scripting language being used.

The actual JavaScript code is placed in the <body> section surrounded by the <script> and </script> tags.

Hello John, welcome to my website. There are 109 days left until Christmas!

```
<html>
    <head>
        <title>
            Christmas Countdown
        </title>
        <script type="text/javascript">
        </script>
    </head>
    <body>
        <script>
            var y=window.prompt("Please enter your name.")
            document.write("Hello "+y+", welcome to my website.");
            //Set the two dates
            today=new Date()
            var christmas=new Date(today.getFullYear(), 11, 25)
            if (today.getMonth()==11 && today.getDate()>25) //if
Christmas has passed already
            christmas.setFullYear(christmas.getFullYear()+1) //
calculate next year's Christmas
            //Set 1 day in milliseconds
            var one_day=1000*60*60*24
            //Calculate difference between the two dates, and
convert to days
            document.write(" There are "+Math.ceil((christmas.
getTime()-today.getTime())/(one_day))+" days left until Christmas!")
        </script>
    </body>
</html>
```

You are expected to know the purpose of JavaScript and be able to give examples of how it can be used to add functionality to websites.

TESTING

Once an information system such as a website or a database has been designed and developed, it should then be tested to detect and remove any errors.

Does the Implementation Match the Design?

A check should be made to ensure that the implementation matches the design so that it contains the correct elements on each page and is free from spelling and grammatical errors.

Links and Navigation

Information systems contain internal and external hyperlinks. They also contain navigation bars and buttons to allow the user to move around the software. All of the links and means of navigation should be tested to ensure that they work properly.

JavaScript

The JavaScript that has been used in an information system to add functionality should be tested to ensure that the code runs correctly.

ONLINE TEST

For a test on scripting and mark-up languages, visit www.brightredbooks.net/N5Computing

 THINGS TO DO AND THINK ABOUT

Try recording macros in Microsoft Word or Excel. For example, you could record the entering of your name in an attractive font. You should then be able to assign your macros to keyboard shortcuts to play them back quickly.

TYPES OF COMPUTER

SUPERCOMPUTER

A **supercomputer** is a very powerful computer that has an extremely high processing speed and massive storage capacity. They are used in applications that require vast amounts of data to be processed quickly, such as weather forecasting, oil and gas exploration and simulations of real situations, such as aeroplanes in wind tunnels and the detonation of nuclear weapons.

Supercomputers are many times the size of a typical desktop computer. They can fill an entire room and require far more electricity to run than desktop and laptop computers. Their high processing capability comes from either combining the processing power of several computers that work together or having a large number of processors that act in parallel on different parts of a complex program at the same time. Supercomputers use massive arrays of hard discs with a typical capacity of several petabytes to store the large amounts of data required by the programs.

DON'T FORGET

Supercomputers can have massive backing store capacities of several petabytes – unlike desktop computers, which have a capacity of 1 or 2 terabytes. Remember that 1 petabyte is equal to 1,024 terabytes.

DESKTOP COMPUTER

A **desktop computer** is a computer that is small enough to sit on a desk but is not easily moved around. They usually do not have their own source of power, so have to stay connected to an electrical socket. Typically, a desktop computer has a QWERTY keyboard with a mouse for input, an LCD, LED or plasma flat screen and a hard disc drive to serve as the main backing store device. Desktop computers with a touchscreen and/or 3D monitor are becoming more widespread. Most desktop computers also have a CD/DVD/Blu-Ray optical drive.

Here is a typical specification of a desktop computer.

Computing hardware is rapidly increasing in speed and capacity, and you should use the Internet and computing magazines to keep up with the current specifications.

Desktop	
Processor speed	3 GHz
RAM capacity	4 GB
Hard disc capacity	1 Tb
Optical drives	CD/DVD/Blu-Ray

DON'T FORGET

The word 'portable' has two different uses in computing. Software is said to be portable if it is easily adapted to run on a different computer system from the one it was originally written for. Hardware is said to be portable if it is easily carried around.

LAPTOP COMPUTER

The main difference between a desktop computer and a **laptop computer** is that laptops are portable. They are therefore suitable for users who wish to work in areas such as a train, a cafe or even the park.

The input/output devices for a laptop include a flat screen, keyboard, and a trackpad or trackball, which serves as the mouse. Solid-state drives are being used increasingly as the backing store for laptop computers, since they have no moving parts and are therefore more resistant to jarring than hard disc drives.

A mouse is not a suitable input device for a laptop computer because there is often not a suitable surface to move it on. However, a mouse can be connected if required through a USB port. Laptops have a battery which allows them to operate without being plugged into a power supply. They include a power adaptor which allows them to recharge the battery.

contd

Early laptops were significantly less powerful than desktop computers, but advances in technology have enabled laptops to perform as well as their desktop counterparts.

Modern laptops often include a wireless networking adaptor to allow users to access the Internet without requiring any wires.

Most laptops cost more than an equivalently powerful desktop computer with a monitor, keyboard and mouse. Also, working long hours on a laptop with a small screen and keyboard can be more tiring than working on a desktop computer.

The specification of a laptop computer is similar to a desktop computer, but in general it will cost more for the same specification.

TABLET COMPUTER

A **tablet computer** is a flat portable computer that is larger than a smartphone and smaller than a laptop, and which uses a touchscreen for input rather than a physical keyboard.

Most tablets support multi-touch input. This allows you to perform actions like pinching an image to zoom in, or opening your fingers to zoom out. To save space, the physical keyboard is replaced by a pop-up keyboard that appears on the screen.

Because of their small size, tablets are very portable and can be easily carried in a small bag.

Tablets offer similar functions to a traditional computer such as word-processing and sending e-mails. However, these tasks can be more difficult without the use of a traditional keyboard and mouse.

SMARTPHONE

A **smartphone** is a mobile phone that includes functions beyond making calls and texting.

Current smartphones have the capability to take photos, play videos and access the Internet. iPhone and Android phones can run small application programs called apps which can provide limitless functionality to the phone. For example, there is a golf app which gives distances from your ball to points on the course such as bunkers, water hazards and the hole. Apps exist which give information on transport timetables and send messages to your phone on when the next bus is due. There are now many thousands of apps available, and the number is increasing rapidly. There is even a Bright Red Revision app available!

Most smartphones have a USB connection, which allow users to upload and download data to and from their computer and update their smartphone software.

THINGS TO DO AND THINK ABOUT

Research the specification of the computers you use at school and at home. Try to find out their processor speed, amount of RAM and hard disc capacity.

ONLINE

Select two scanners from websites such as PC World, Currys and Dell and compare their specification and cost. Repeat the process for two inkjet printers.

ONLINE TEST

For a test on types of computers, visit www.brightredbooks.net/N5Computing

INPUT AND OUTPUT DEVICES

INPUT DEVICES

Input devices are used to enter data into a computer system. A keyboard and mouse are commonly used to enter text, but there are a wide variety of other input devices to enter graphics, video and sound into a computer system.

Keyboard (QWERTY)

A keyboard is the main method used by computer users to enter text into a computer system. Early mechanical typewriters used an arrangement of keys to prevent keys from jamming which is still used by virtually all keyboards today. The term **QWERTY** keyboard refers to the arrangement of the first six letters on the top left corner of the keyboard.

Mouse

A **mouse** is used to move a pointer and select options on the screen.

Touchpad

A **touchpad** does the same job as a mouse but uses your finger on a small pad to move the pointer and make selections.

Scanner

A **scanner** is used to capture images by scanning an image and converting it into digital data so that it can be entered into a computer. Most scanners are flatbed, which means that they have a flat scanning surface.

The resolution of a scanner is measured in dots per inch (d.p.i.). Typically, a scanner has a resolution of a few thousand dots per inch.

Digital Camera

Digital cameras capture pictures by converting the light emitted by the image into digital data that can be stored on flash memory cards. This means that unwanted pictures can be easily deleted without the wastage of film which would have happened with old-fashioned analogue cameras. An average-capacity flash card can store many thousands of pictures.

Current **digital cameras** have a typical resolution of around 15 megapixels, which means that they can capture 15 million dots of light to store an image.

Digital Camcorder

A digital camcorder captures video data as a series of bit-map graphics frames per second. A typical capture rate is 30 frames per second. High-resolution and colour video files are very high-capacity. Video data can also be captured by mobile phones and webcams.

Graphics Tablet

A **graphics tablet** is used to enter graphics by writing on a horizontal surface with a special pen called a stylus. This is more natural and much easier than drawing with a mouse.

Touch-Sensitive Screen

Touchscreens accept input by detecting human touch on an electronic grid. Early touch-screens accepted only a single point of input, but they have developed to input multi-finger motions to perform actions such as zooming in/out and rotation.

ONLINE

Look at websites such as PC World or Dell to keep up to date on developments in computing input and output devices and their specification and cost.

contd

Joystick

A **joystick** is used primarily as an input device in video games. It is a stick that can be moved in different directions to control the movement of an object on the screen. A button on the top of the joystick can be used to act as a trigger or for some other function.

Microphone

A **microphone** in conjunction with a sound card is used to capture sound. The microphone senses the sound energy, and then a sound card is used to convert it into a form that can be entered into a computer system.

OUTPUT DEVICES

Inkjet Printer

An **inkjet printer** works by spraying thousands of tiny droplets of quick-drying ink onto paper as it is fed through the printer. The speed and resolution can be very good, but there is a running cost of ink cartridges which can overtake the initial cost of the printer.

Laser Printer

Laser printers work by using a laser to make an electric charge of the image on the surface of a cylindrical drum. A toner cartridge is then used to coat the drum with powder which sticks to the areas that have been charged by the laser. The toner is then transferred to the paper to form the image to paper.

Laser printers produce good-quality images and are very fast but are much more expensive than inkjet printers.

Monitor

Early desktop computers used a **CRT** (Cathode Ray Tube) **monitor** which was heavy and bulky. These have now been replaced by flat screens such as **LCD** (Liquid Crystal Display), which uses less power, and **TFT** (Thin Film Transistor), where the pixels of the display are created with tiny transistors.

Plasma screens are another type of flat-panel display. The display is produced by small cells containing tiny fluorescent lamps that can change colour.

Flat-Bed Plotter

A **flat-bed plotter** draws an image using a pen on a horizontal sheet of paper. They are used to produce large-scale technical drawings where accuracy is important, and in general they are much more expensive than printers.

Loudspeaker

A **loudspeaker** in conjunction with a sound card is used to output sound. The sound card converts the digital data in the computer into a form that can generate sound on the speakers.

 DON'T FORGET

Don't confuse storage devices with input and output devices. A storage device such as a hard disc drive inputs data from the disc when a file is opened and outputs data to the disc when a file is saved. However, the main purpose of a hard disc is to store files permanently, and so it should be referred to as a storage device and not as an input or output device.

 THINGS TO DO AND THINK ABOUT

You should keep up to date on the specifications of computer hardware. Get into the habit of acquiring computing magazines, and familiarise yourself with the resolution, capacity, speed and cost of digital cameras, scanners, printers, laptops and so on.

 ONLINE TEST

For a test on input and output devices, log onto www.brightredbooks.net/ N5Computing

STORAGE DEVICES

INTRODUCTION

When a computer is switched off, the contents of main memory are lost unless they have been saved to a permanent storage device. **Storage devices** such as hard drives and USB flash drives are used to keep a permanent copy of program and data files. Most storage devices have a high capacity to store substantial amounts of data.

The capacity of a storage device is the amount of data that can be stored on the device and is usually measured in gigabytes or terabytes.

The speed of a storage device is a measure of how fast data can be written to or read from the device. Data can be read at a faster speed than it can be written, since writing involves making a physical change to the material of the device to encode the data.

TYPES OF STORAGE DEVICES: MAGNETIC

Magnetic storage devices include hard disc drives and magnetic tape drives. They are called magnetic storage devices because their recording surfaces are coated with a material that enables data to be stored digitally by using different forms of magnetisation.

Hard disc drive

Hard discs are used as the main backing storage device on a computer. Most desktop computers have a built-in hard disc drive, but external hard disc drives are now commonly available to make backup copies and to transfer data between computers. External drives can be connected to the computer with a cable to the USB port.

The read/write head on a hard disc can go straight to any point on the surface of the disc. This type of access to data is fast and is called **direct access** or **random access**. Modern hard disc drives can have a capacity of several terabytes.

Magnetic tape drive

Magnetic tape is mostly used for making backup copies of large amounts of data. This device has to wind through other data on the tape to find the required data. This type of access to data is slow and is called **sequential access**. The highest-capacity tape cartridges can store several terabytes of data and are relatively cheap.

 DON'T FORGET

Don't confuse the terms 'device' and 'medium'. The device is the complete mechanical unit, whereas the medium is the material on which the data is recorded. For example, the device could be a disc drive or a magnetic tape drive, and the medium is a hard disc or a magnetic tape.

TYPES OF STORAGE DEVICES: OPTICAL

Optical storage devices include CD-ROM, CD-R, CD-RW, DVD-ROM, DVD-RW and Blu-Ray.

They all use laser technology to store and retrieve data by burning areas on a disc to create pits and lands to encode data. All of these discs can be used to store computer data. DVDs (Digital Versatile Disc) and Blu-Ray discs are used to store feature-length films because their higher capacity allows the storage of large amounts of multimedia data.

A CD (Compact Disc) stores approximately 800 Mb, a DVD approximately 5 GB and Blu-Ray approximately 25 GB.

TYPES OF STORAGE DEVICES: SOLID STATE

Solid-state storage devices have no moving parts and are made up entirely from electronic components. Memory cards (flash cards) are used in digital cameras, digital video cameras and mobile phones to store and transfer data.

USB flash memory sticks are high-capacity storage devices that can be used to backup data and transfer data easily between computers.

Memory sticks and memory cards typically have a capacity of 4, 8, 16 or 32 gigabytes.

INTERFACE

A computer's processor can execute thousands of millions of instructions per second. Peripheral devices have different operational characteristics and operate at a slower speed than the processor.

An interface is the hardware and software required between a processor and a peripheral device, to compensate for the differences in their speeds and the way in which they operate.

An interface performs the following functions.

1   Physical connection
    A physical link between the peripheral and the processor.

2   Data storage
    Data is temporarily stored in an area of memory called a buffer until the device is ready to deal with it.

3   Data format conversion
    Voltage conversion – the peripheral devices may operate at different voltages from the CPU.

    Serial-to-parallel conversion – some peripheral devices transfer data in serial (1 bit after another down one line), whereas the processor transfers data in parallel (several lines are used to transfer the data).

THINGS TO DO AND THINK ABOUT

Storage devices can be classified as optical, magnetic and solid-state. The suitability of a storage device for a given situation will depend on factors such as its cost, capacity, access speed and portability.

Use the website www.pcworld.co.uk to research the cost, capacity and access speed of an actual Blu-Ray drive, hard disc drive and USB memory stick.

Put the data into a table and write a paragraph comparing the devices.

HARDWARE AND OPERATING SYSTEM REQUIREMENTS

INTRODUCTION

An information system has **hardware** and **software** requirements to allow it to be run. There must be enough storage capacity and speed of access as well as an operating system that will provide a platform for the application. The system must have input and output devices with the necessary characteristics. For example, the screen must be capable of displaying the correct resolution. Also the hardware, operating system and applications must all be compatible with each other.

An application software package will include details of the minimum system specification required to run the application.

Shown below are the minimum system requirements for Access 2012, which is a database application.

1	Minimum processor speed	500 megahertz (MHz) or higher
2	Minimum RAM	256 Mb
3	Minimum hard disc space	2 Gb
4	Display	1,024 x 768
5	Operating system	Windows XP or later

ONLINE

The software applications that you use at school and at home will have a minimum requirements specification that is recommended by the manufacturers.
Try to find out the requirements of some of these applications by looking up the manufacturer's site on the Internet.

HARDWARE

The hardware requirements for a system are usually specified for the processor, main memory and hard disc. Some systems require specialised input and output devices which will also have a minimum requirements specification.

Processor Type and Speed

The processor must be fast enough to run the software and must also be compatible with the operating system. Manufacturers produce families of processors that are compatible with a range of operating-system versions. The minimum speed will be capable of running the application but will often be very slow, and a faster processor may be required to give a reasonable performance.

Memory (RAM, ROM)

Software will normally specify a minimum RAM requirement but may also recommend more for enhanced performance. For example, an audio recorder may require a minimum of 96 Mb to run, but may use 512 Mb to allow for greater sampling rates to produce higher-quality sound or to add special effects to enhance the sound.

Some applications such as video-editing have large files which require a lot of RAM into which they must be loaded to be edited.

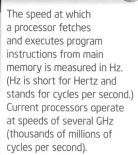

DON'T FORGET

The speed at which a processor fetches and executes program instructions from main memory is measured in Hz. (Hz is short for Hertz and stands for cycles per second.) Current processors operate at speeds of several GHz (thousands of millions of cycles per second).

contd

Hard Disc

RAM is used to temporarily store the application and data files when the program is being executed. However, sometimes it is important to consider the backing store for applications that generate large data files. The capacity of the hard disc is therefore important but also the speed of access, since some applications require large data files to be loaded up from the hard disc when the application is running. If the access speed is too slow, then the program can run with unacceptable delays to the user each time the program needs to access data from the hard disc.

OPERATING SYSTEM

An operating system is a large program that manages the hardware and software of a computing system.

There are several **operating systems** each with a large number of versions. Windows, Apple OS and Linux are examples of operating systems which have been developed for desktop and laptop computers.

A software package which runs on one of these operating systems will not run on another without being modified. Also, software which runs on one version of an operating system will often not run on a more up-to-date version.

Incompatibilities arise because any application program needs to communicate with the operating system to perform basic actions such as entering data, printing and saving files to disc. Therefore an **application package** that has been written to communicate with one version of an operating system will sometimes not work properly with a later version.

A device driver is a program that allows a peripheral device to communicate with the application that uses the device. Most drivers come with the operating system, but some may need a new driver to be installed when the device is connected to the computer. There are problems with drivers because computer manufacturers use different hardware from each other and therefore require different drivers to be installed. This can mean that a particular software application will run on one computer and not on another due to incompatibilities with the device drivers.

 THINGS TO DO AND THINK ABOUT

An application program has technical issues in terms of the hardware and software requirements for it to be run. Processor speed, memory capacity and the operating-system platform requirements all have to be considered. As advances are made in hardware technology, the minimum requirements are increasing.

 **DON'T FORGET**

Apart from the hard disc, other storage devices can be important to the system. For example, files may be required to be stored on a portable storage device such as a CD or DVD for distribution.

 ONLINE TEST

Test your knowledge of hardware and operating-system requirements at www.brightredbooks.net/N5Computing

COMPUTER NETWORKS

STAND-ALONE OR NETWORKED

A **stand-alone computer** is one that is not connected to any other computers. A **networked computer** is one which is connected to one or more other computers. Networked computers are fitted with a NIC (Network Interface Card). The NIC is a circuit board that has a unique address to identify the computer on the network and converts the signals from the computer into a form that can be transmitted over the network.

TRANSMISSION MEDIA

The **transmission media** is the type of connection used to link the computers together. The media used to transfer data can be electrical wires, optical fibres or wireless connections.

Bandwidth is a term used to describe the speed of data transfer. It measures how much data can be sent over a connection in a given amount of time.

Wired media include **Unshielded Twisted Pair** (UTP), which is a low-cost but low-bandwidth media, and **coaxial cable**, which is more expensive but is better shielded against interference and has a faster bandwidth.

Optical fibres use glass threads to transmit the data in the form of light waves. They have a much higher bandwidth than electrical cables, which means that they are used on networks which carry a high volume of data. Optical fibre cables are less susceptible than electrical cables to interference and are much thinner and lighter.

Wireless connections use radio and microwaves to transfer data between computers instead of conventional physical wired connections. Wireless connections are slower than physical connections but save money in cabling and make it easier to move the computers around.

This table shows typical bandwidths provided by different transmission media.

Media	Bandwidth
UTP	100 Mbps
Coaxial cable	600 Mbps
Optical fibre	1 GBps
Wireless	50 Mbps

DON'T FORGET

Bandwidth is measured in bits per second rather than bytes per second. Mbps stands for megabits per second, and GBps stands for gigabits per second. Don't get mixed up with megabytes and gigabytes, which are units of capacity.

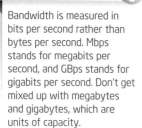

PEER-TO-PEER AND CLIENT/SERVER

A **peer-to-peer network** is a cheap, small-scale computer network suited to a family home or a small office, where all the computers have equal status. Each computer can access files on the other computers and share peripherals such as printers without the need for a central file server to store files.

Security is poor on a peer-to-peer network since there is no easy way of allocating different levels of access rights to users.

Other disadvantages are that software has to be installed on each of the individual machines, and backups of data are difficult since it is spread over several machines and not stored centrally on a file server.

In a **client/server network**, the computers do not all have the same status. Computers are operating either as a server which provides a network resource, or as a client which makes use of the network resources.

The functions provided by servers include file servers, which store and control access to files, and print servers, which manage the sending of files to printers.

contd

The client/server networks have good security by controlling access to files on the file server, and backups are easy since users' files are stored centrally. Software has to be installed only once on the file server and then allocated to the clients.

	Peer-to-Peer	Client/Server
Cost	Cheap	Expensive
Size of network	Small-scale	Medium to large
Security	Poor	Very good
Backups	Difficult	Easy

LAN (LOCAL-AREA NETWORK)

A **LAN** is a computer network that is located in a relatively small area such as a school or an office building. The picture shows an example of a star topology in which each client is linked to a central file server with their own connection.

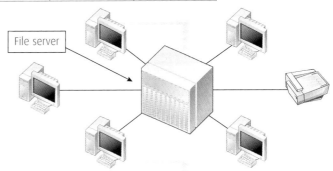

File server

INTERNET

The **Internet** is a global computer network that consists of LANs and individual computers all connected up together. The **World Wide Web** (WWW) is a vast amount of **multimedia** information stored on websites on server computers on the Internet. Websites can be accessed by entering their address into a browser or by entering appropriate keywords into a search engine.

Early computers used a **dial-up connection**, which required a new connection to be made for each session and had a very slow bandwidth. This has been replaced by a **broadband connection**, which is always on and has a bandwidth that is hundreds of times faster than a dial-up connection. Dial-up operated in Kbps, whereas a broadband connection provides speeds in tens of Mbps.

An **ISP** (Internet Service Provider) is a company that provides a connection to the Internet and allows the user to be online.

ONLINE

For a full explanation of how the Internet works, follow the link at www.brightredbooks.net/N5Computing

CLOUD STORAGE

The data on individual computers and computer networks is typically stored on hard disc drives, with USB memory sticks and optical discs being used to make backup copies.

Cloud storage is a different type of storage in that it uses online services to store large amounts of data on the Internet or a remote computer network. It is called cloud storage because the Internet is sometimes represented in diagrams as a cloud. Cloud storage provides a secure way of remotely storing important data.

An individual could use cloud storage to store personal e-mails and photo files, or a large company could keep a backup copy of all of their network data.

One advantage of cloud storage compared to storing data locally is that data can be accessed from any computer in the world provided that it has an Internet link. Another advantage is that cloud storage makes available an almost unlimited storage capacity, which is not the case for a computer's hard disc drive. However, downloading and uploading large amounts of data can be slow depending upon the speed of the Internet connection, and if the Internet connection goes down then no data can be accessed.

DON'T FORGET

Cloud storage is also called web storage, since it uses the World Wide Web to store data.

ONLINE TEST

Test your knowledge of hardware and operating system requirements at www.brightredbooks.net/N5Computing

THINGS TO DO AND THINK ABOUT

Look into the network used in your own school. Try to find out from your teacher how the network is managed and what network devices and transmission media are used.

SECURITY RISKS 1

WHAT IS PHISHING?

Phishing is a scam carried out by hackers that uses a false website to gather personal information from unsuspecting users. The website will often imitate a legitimate website such as eBay, PayPal or e-mail sites. The false website can ask the user to enter details such as their name, address, phone number, social-security number and credit-card number. These details can then be used in fraudulent activities to gain money or purchase goods at the expense of the user who has unwittingly provided their details.

Spotting Phishing

Professional **hackers** will be very careful and create a false website that looks virtually identical to the original, but others are poor counterfeits and can be spotted if you know what to look for. Poor phishing attempts will contain some or all of the following:

- Spelling and grammatical errors – many phishing sites can be identified by misspellings and grammatical errors.

- Poor-quality graphics – often the images in the site are of a low resolution and not as clear as you would expect in a professional website.

- Poorly designed website – legitimate companies have websites that are developed and maintained by highly trained website developers. Phishing sites can have an amateur feel to them, with poor layout of text and images, as they are not designed to the same level of quality that you would expect from a large company.

- Asking you to send sensitive data – legitimate sites would not ask you to send your password, account details or other sensitive data by e-mail. This is usually a sign of fraud. Contacting the website by telephone or some other means is a way of seeing whether the website is valid.

- Non-specific e-mails – a legitimate company would correspond by e-mail with mention of the user's name or some other kind of identification. A fraudulent e-mail will often use more general terms to address the person, such as 'user', 'customer' or 'client'.

- Incorrect information – an e-mail containing information that is noticeably incorrect could be a sign that it is a phishing e-mail.

- Unrelated links – an e-mail from a bank will not include an advertisement for pharmaceuticals, nor should the links in the e-mail take you to any place but the company's actual website. E-mails that contain potentially real information alongside information you'd see in junk e-mails are usually phishing attempts.

VIDEO

Watch the Youtube video 'Symantec Guide to Scary Internet Stuff – Phishing' at www.brightredbooks.net/N5Computing

DON'T FORGET

The term 'phishing' comes from the word 'fishing'. This is because in a sense the hacker is fishing for your personal details in the hope that you will take the bait.

KEYLOGGING

A keylogger is an item of software that records the keys that the user presses on a computer keyboard. Keylogger programs are intended to be used to help to identify technical problems and to monitor employees but can also be used maliciously to steal personal data including usernames, passwords and other private information. Employers can use keylogger programs to monitor the activities of workers in a company to make sure that they are not wasting time on the company network by playing games, e-mailing friends, booking holidays and so on.

Keylogger programs can be identified and removed by **anti-virus software**.

SPYWARE

This is software that, once installed on your computer, can 'spy' on your activities. This could involve making a record of which websites you have visited, capturing your e-mail messages or getting hold of your private information such as passwords and credit-card details.

Utility programs called anti-spyware can be used to search for and remove spyware from a computer system.

ONLINE

Use a search engine to research further information on phishing, keylogging and spyware.

IDENTITY THEFT

Criminals can steal your identity by finding out your personal details on computer systems and then using this information to open bank accounts, credit cards, loans and documents such as passports and driving licences in your name.

DON'T FORGET

Security is a huge problem with the Internet and computer networks. You should be aware not only of the risks but also the steps that can be taken to protect against and minimise the risk.

ONLINE FRAUD

This is any type of fraud scheme that uses the Internet to unlawfully obtain money and property. Examples are the non-delivery of paid-for goods, transactions carried out with stolen credit/debit cards and bad-cheque scams. Each year, online fraud costs the UK economy tens of billions of pounds. The amount of fraud is increasing, and banks and other companies are spending large amounts of money to protect themselves against this type of crime.

ONLINE TEST

For a test on security risks, log on to www.brightredbooks.net/N5Computing

THINGS TO DO AND THINK ABOUT

Imagine you are put in charge of Internet security at a big company. What measures would you put into place to prevent secure information from being stolen by hackers?

SECURITY RISKS 2

HACKING

Hacking is the process of unlawfully breaking into computer systems to gain access to private and confidential information. Some people think that hacking is fun and very clever – but it is a criminal activity, and many hackers are put in prison for their crimes. The hacker will often gain access to online computer systems from a remote computer, which makes him/her hard to catch. The hacker may just look at confidential information and not change the data, but can also more seriously make changes to data such as bank-account balances and electricity bills.

Hackers have gained access to computer systems of organisations such as eBay, the US military, international banks and telecommunications companies.

VIRUSES

A **virus** is a program that enters a computer (usually without the knowledge of the user) and performs some annoying or harmful action. It is called a virus because it is similar to a medical virus which infects a human being, in that it infects the host and spreads to other hosts. A computer virus will damage the healthy operation of the computer and can replicate itself and then spread to other computers. The most common mechanism for viruses spreading is through e-mails. The effect of being infected by a computer virus can vary from a relatively harmless activity, such as displaying unwanted messages on the screen, to deleting files from memory or even preventing the computer from starting up again.

WORMS

A **worm** is similar to a virus in that it is a program that causes harm to the infected computer. Unlike a virus, the main function of a worm is to replicate itself and also to spread automatically from computer to computer. For example, a worm could send a copy of itself to everyone in an e-mail address book. The worm then replicates and sends itself to everyone listed in each receiver's address book. In this way, a worm can spread very quickly and cause damage to thousands or even millions of people.

By replication itself, a worm can clog up the memory of a computer and can cause the response of a computer to slow down or grind to a halt. As its name implies, a worm can also tunnel down deeply into folders, which can make it very hard to detect and remove.

TROJANS

A **Trojan** is named after the Trojan horse in Greek mythology, which allowed the Greeks to enter the city of Troy by hiding inside a large wooden horse which was presented to the Trojans as a gift. In computing, a Trojan is a piece of software which, when installed on a user's machine, creates a back door on a computer that gives malicious users access to the files stored on the computer. Trojans often pretend to be legitimate files presented as gifts in an attempt to persuade users to download them and install them on their computer.

DON'T FORGET

The word Trojan should always be spelt with a capital 'T' and not a small 't', because it refers to the ancient country of Troy.

DENIAL-OF-SERVICE ATTACK (DOS ATTACK)

A **denial-of-service attack** is one in which a company's network servers, or resources including hard disc drive and network connections, are put under pressure in a way that prevents legitimate users from being able to use the network resources.

An example is an attack against a server computer on a network in which it is flooded with data by other computers over the Internet, which results in the server being unable to perform its usual functions.

Costs of Denial-of-Service Attacks

The victim of a DoS attack can incur costs due to the loss of business during the downtime caused by the attack. It could be a matter of hours or even days to recover from an attack.

There are also costs of repairing the damage and getting the network functioning properly again.

Reasons for Denial-of-Service Attacks

Some attacks are performed by companies or governments to try to cause harm to their competitors. For example, the US White House website suffered a DoS attack after the Chinese embassy in Belgrade was accidentally bombed.

Some attacks are carried out for personal reasons. For example, a disgruntled employee who believes that he/she has been unfairly dismissed can mount an attack against his/her former company's network.

Some DoS attacks are merely malicious. They are performed by individuals who see such activities as good fun, although this does not make them any less damaging or inconvenient to the target network.

ONLINE

The Internet contains a large number of sites on this topic. Enter 'DoS attacks' into a search engine and investigate further.

DON'T FORGET

DoS (Denial of Service) is an example of an acronym. There are a lot of acronyms used in computing. An acronym is a new 'word' formed by combining the first letter of each word in a phrase. Make sure that you know the expansions of the acronyms used in this course.

ONLINE TEST

Test yourself on security risks at www.brightredbooks.net/N5Computing

THINGS TO DO AND THINK ABOUT

Viruses, worms and Trojans are examples of malware which refers to software program that are designed to do harm or other unwanted actions to a computer system. The word 'malware' literally means bad software.

SECURITY PRECAUTIONS

ANTI-VIRUS SOFTWARE

Anti-virus software scans a computer system to detect and remove viruses. Viruses can be identified if they have a known pattern of instructions or if the virus program is performing some suspicious activity such as copying the contents of an e-mail address book in order to spread to other computers. Since new viruses are constantly being created, it is important to regularly update the anti-virus software so that it will recognise these new viruses. Many anti-virus software programs also protect against other types of harmful software such as **spyware** and **adware** which can irritatingly display advertisements on your computer.

PASSWORDS, ENCRYPTION AND BIOMETRICS

Passwords

User accounts on networks and stand-alone computers can be protected with **passwords**. Usually, a username is required to log on, as well as a password to provide extra security. Individual files such as word-processing and spreadsheet documents can also be given a password which is needed to open the file.

Some passwords are case-sensitive, which means that the password distinguishes between uppercase and lowercase letters.

Passwords should be chosen wisely so that it is hard for other people to discover or guess your password. Using a mixture of random uppercase letters, lowercase letters, digits and punctuation characters makes for a strong password. Some people pick weak passwords such as the name of their pet, friend, football team and so on, or a password that is too short and is easily discovered by other people who can then hack into their account. For example, the password R3jK942f is much stronger than the password Vegas.

DON'T FORGET

It is important to change your password regularly. If it is stolen, there will then be less time in which it can be used to access your private information or to do damage.

contd

Encryption

Encryption is protecting data by putting it into code so that it can't be understood if it is accessed. Secure websites and sensitive data such as passwords are encrypted so that they can't be read without the correct decoding key.

Biometrics

This is a form of security system based on the detection and recognition of human physical characteristics. Common examples are retinal scans, fingerprints and voice and face recognition. These characteristics are unique to a human being and so are very difficult to forge. Some systems require the input of a username and password as well as some form of **biometric** scan to provide extra security.

SECURITY PROTOCOLS AND FIREWALLS

Security Protocols

When data is transmitted from one computer to another over the Internet or any computer network, it is important that the data is kept secure. **Security protocols** are an agreement between the sender and the receiver about how the data is sent so that a successful and secure exchange can take place. This can involve authentication of the user's identity, encoding of sensitive details such as credit-card numbers and ensuring that the data has not been tampered with. **HTTPS** (HyperText Transfer Protocol Secure) is a protocol used by organisations such as banks and companies involved in e-commerce on their websites to transfer data securely over the Internet.

Firewalls

A **firewall** protects a computer system from damage from unauthorised users by filtering all incoming and outgoing Internet traffic through a firewall computer. It does this by analysing the packets of data being transmitted and determining whether they should be allowed through or not. Thus only known and trusted users are permitted to access the data on the computer system. Firewalls can also control which websites a computer can access on the Internet.

Individual home computers can be protected with a firewall to improve security on the Internet. Companies will protect their networks using a network firewall.

SECURITY SUITES

A **security suite** is a group of utility programs that protect a computer from viruses and other malware. Anti-virus software and firewalls are the main functions of most security suites. However, other functions are usually provided such as parental controls, protection against identity theft, and password protection of data storage.

Some security suites offer more types of protection than others which are limited in their protection. It is also important that the security suite is updated regularly to guard against the latest malware threats.

ONLINE

Research the functions provided by different types of security suites on the Internet. Norton and McAfee are two companies that make security suites.

THINGS TO DO AND THINK ABOUT

There are many threats to the security of a computer system from which the users need to be protected. These include threats from viruses, hackers and protecting children from access to unwanted material on the Internet. Passwords, encryption, biometrics, security protocols and firewalls are different means of protecting a computer system and keeping the data being held secure.

ONLINE TEST

Test yourself on security precautions at www. brightredbooks.net/ N5Computing

LEGAL IMPLICATIONS

DATA PROTECTION ACT

In the modern world, organisations such as companies, governments, sports clubs and medical centres hold personal data on people in databases and other information systems. The **Data Protection Act** was introduced in 1984 to protect the rights of individuals in society against misuse of their data being held on computer systems and networks.

The **data subjects** are the people whose information is being stored. The **data users** are the people in the organisation who need to use the data to run the business. For example, in a dentist's practice, the data subjects would be the patients and the data users would be the dentists and secretaries.

Requirements of the Data Protection Act

The main requirements of this act are:

- An organisation intending to hold data must register with a central government agency.

- Individuals can demand a print-out of their data to see exactly what data is being held on them. (Such requests cannot be made to the police and national security departments of government.)

- Data on individuals that is no longer required must be deleted. For example, if someone closed a bank account or left a golf club, then the organisation should remove their details from their databases.

- Measures should be taken to keep the data secure, such as passwords and physical security provided by locks and keys.

- The data being held should be accurate and up to date.

DON'T FORGET

It is common for students to mix up the Data Protection Act with the Computer Misuse Act. Be clear that the Data Protection Act is about protecting individuals so that their data is used for the proper purposes, whereas the Computer Misuse Act is about guarding against harmful activities such as spreading computer viruses and hacking.

COMPUTER MISUSE ACT

This Act was introduced in 1990 to protect against criminals who perform destructive actions and invasions of privacy on computer systems.

Activities Covered by the Computer Misuse Act

The main activities covered by the **Computer Misuse Act** are:

- It is illegal to send computer viruses to perform harm to computer systems.

- It is unlawful to hack into computer systems to gain private and confidential information.

COPYRIGHT, DESIGNS AND PATENTS ACT

This law gives rights to the developers of computer software so that their work is not copied or adapted for use without the permission of the creators. The **Copyright, Designs and Patents Act** also covers the illegal copying of music, films, images, manuscripts and so on stored on a computer.

Over the last decade, there have been rapid technological advances in storage devices and networking which have made it easier to store and transfer unlawful copies of files over the Internet. The music and film industries lose billions of pounds each year to music and film piracy.

HEALTH-AND-SAFETY REGULATIONS

There are several dangers to your health and safety when using a computer at work or at home. Employers have a legal responsibility to take steps to try to avoid potential problems. For example, workers have a right to regular breaks to avoid some of the problems that can occur when doing work on a computer all day long.

Safe Computer Use

Sitting at a computer for lengthy periods of time can cause backache and neckache. These problems can be avoided with a well-designed workspace and a comfortable seat that allows for good posture.

Screen glare can cause headaches and deterioration of eyesight over long periods of time. The use of screen filters which are placed over the screen is one means of addressing this issue.

Some people spend most of their time at work typing data into a computer. This can cause hand and wrist pain and even arthritis over time. Repetitive Strain Injury (RSI) is a term used to describe the pain and injury caused by repetitive movement and overuse of muscles in this kind of way.

There are also potential dangers caused by cabling and electric plugs. Too many plugs in one socket can cause overheating and can sometimes catch fire. Loose cables or cables lying on floors can be tripped over and cause damaging falls to the people using the computers.

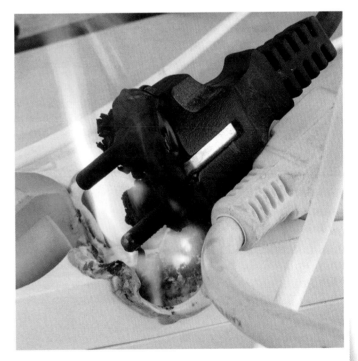

 ONLINE TEST

For a test on the legal implications associated with the use of computers, visit www.brightredbooks.net/N5Computing

COMMUNICATIONS ACT

This Act covers the improper use of public electronic communications networks such as the Internet or mobile phone networks. Under this Act it is an offence to send messages or other material that is grossly offensive or of an indecent nature. Cyberbullying which involves the abuse of technology to harass or threaten others is covered by this Act.

 ONLINE

Go to the government website (find the link at www.brightredbooks.net/N5Computing) and enter 'Safe Computer Use' into the 'Search this site' text box. Use this site to investigate further health-and-safety problems and how to reduce their risk.

 THINGS TO DO AND THINK ABOUT

There are four areas of legislation you should know about for this course. Make sure that you know the EXACT name of each act and not an abbreviated or misspelt version such as 'The Copyright Act'.

ENVIRONMENTAL IMPACT

ENERGY USE

How much electricity do computers use?

A typical **desktop computer** uses about 100 to 250 watts, which is considerably more than a laptop computer, which uses around 20 to 60 watts. If a computer is on the Internet and making intensive use of its processor and disc drives, then it will consume much more energy than a computer that is offline and performing tasks that are less demanding of the system. It can be calculated that a typical desktop computer being used for 8 hours a day would use about 500 kilowatt hours in one year. At a current cost of around 10p per kilowatt hour, this would amount to a cost of £50 a year.

Go to the website www.electricity-usage.com and use the calculator to explore how much energy your computer and peripheral devices use.

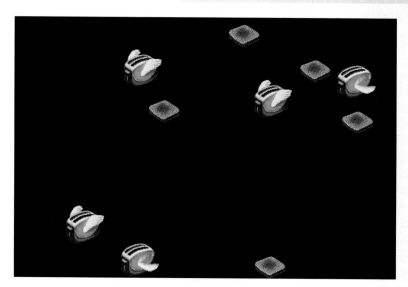

Screensavers

At one time, certain areas of the screen got 'burned' by showing the same display when the computer was not in use. A screensaver is designed to 'save' the screen when a computer is not being used by displaying random images which move around the screen. In this way, no particular area of the screen becomes 'burnt'. At one time, screensavers with elaborate moving patterns such as flying toasters were very popular, but it is now accepted that screensavers are not such a good idea because they use up some energy even when the computer is not being used.

Sleep Mode

The energy requirements of computers can be reduced by putting them into 'sleep or standby mode' when they are not being used. This substantially reduces the power being used by the computer without closing the programs currently being run.

Peripheral devices attached to a computer also require additional power to operate. Turning off or unplugging peripherals such as scanners and printers when not in use can also help to reduce the amount of energy being consumed.

The following table indicates a comparison of energy use for different types of computer systems and how they are being used.

More Energy	Less Energy
Ready to be used	Sleep or Standby mode
Desktop	Laptop
Faster processor	Slower processor
Older processor (e.g. Pentium)	Newer processor (Core Duo)
PC	Mac
Heavy use (e.g. all drives in use, processor-intensive task)	Light use (e.g. e-mail, word-processing)
On the Internet	Offline

DISPOSAL OF IT EQUIPMENT

Computing technology is constantly improving, which means that a state-of-the-art computer bought today will be out of date in a few years' time. Therefore computers, mobile phones, peripheral devices and so on are frequently disposed of in order to make way for newer models. The problem then arises of how to dispose of these unwanted items. Computers are made up of plastic, glass and steel and chemicals such as mercury, lead and cadmium. If these computers are just thrown away, then there are serious consequences for pollution of the environment and contamination of the water we drink and the air we breathe.

One partial solution is to recycle many of the materials used in computers, which can help to save resources and protect the environment.

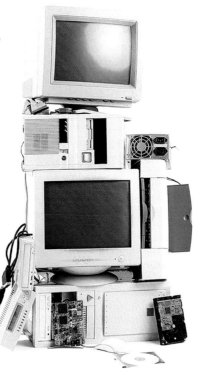

VIDEO LINK

Watch the video on 'How to recycle computers' at www.brightredbooks.net/N5Computing

CARBON FOOTPRINT

There is some debate about how much greenhouse gases are contributing to global warming. However, it is generally accepted that emissions of **greenhouse gases**, in particular carbon dioxide, make a serious contribution to climate change.

Carbon footprint is a measure of how much carbon dioxide is produced in the making or use of devices such as televisions, cars, aircraft and computing equipment.

The manufacture of IT equipment contributes to the carbon footprint. The making of a single desktop computer requires the burning of 10 times its own weight in fossil fuel.

Using computing equipment uses electricity, which is largely produced in power stations by burning fossil fuels such as coal and oil. The waste product of this process is the creation of large amounts of carbon dioxide.

On the other hand, in some respects the use of IT can help to reduce the carbon footprint. For example, the increasing number of people working from home decreases the need for travel. Cars, buses and trains all burn a large amount of fossil fuels.

Another example is that of **video conferencing**, where meetings take place in a virtual conference using online computers and multimedia hardware devices. Traditional meetings in hotels and conference centres can require air travel, which has a large carbon footprint.

DON'T FORGET

Apart from carbon dioxide, there are other gases that contribute towards climate change. Nitrogen trifluoride (NF_3) is produced as a waste product by factories that make flat-screen displays. This gas is more harmful in warming the atmosphere than carbon dioxide but is produced in much smaller amounts.

THINGS TO DO AND THINK ABOUT

The manufacture, use and disposal of IT hardware have consequences for the environment. They use up the world's resources, cause pollution and leave a carbon footprint which is contributing towards global warming. Steps to reduce these effects include developing computers that consume less energy and the recycling of hardware components. Look around your house or classroom and identify things that you already do or could improve on to reduce your energy use.

ONLINE TEST

Test yourself on the environmental impact of computing online at www.brightredbooks.net/N5Computing

OUTCOMES AND UNIT ASSESSMENT

INTRODUCTION

Each of the two mandatory units (Software Design and Development; Information System Design and Development) requires you to achieve an assessment standard in a set of learning outcomes.

In the Information System Design and Development unit, there are two learning outcomes.

These are listed below.

OUTCOMES

Outcome 1

Develop one or more information systems, using appropriate development tools such as databases or websites.

Outcome 2

Consider the factors involved in the design and implementation of an information system by describing its hardware and software requirements, security risks, impact on the environment and so on.

DETAILS OF THE OUTCOMES

Each of the two learning outcomes has several parts. All of the subsections must be achieved to gain a pass for the outcome.

Outcome 1

This is a practical outcome in which you have to achieve each of the following criteria through the development of one or more information systems.

1.1 Creating a structure and links

1.2 Creating a user interface

1.3 Writing or editing simple code

1.4 Integrating different media types

1.5 Identifying and rectifying errors.

The links can be achieved through internal and external hyperlinks in a website, links between slides or to files in a presentation, or links between records and files in a database.

contd

Your information system must allow the user to input choices and navigate through the system. For example, a website could have a navigation bar to move around the different web pages. Text should be used to inform the user of the result of any actions such as 'Go to first page', 'Undo', 'Play video' and so on.

Databases and websites have scripting languages that allow you to add extra functionality to the software. For example, you could be using VBA (Visual Basic for Applications) with an Access database, or you could be using JavaScript with a website.

The information system must use a combination of text, graphics, video and sound media types. The different types of media can be stored in text, graphics, video and sound files which can then be imported directly into databases, presentations and websites.

You are expected to identify and remove any errors from the software. It is easy not to spot errors in something that you wrote yourself. It is a good idea to get another student to test out your information system who might discover problems that you would know how to avoid.

Outcome 2

This is a written outcome in which you have to consider each of the following factors in respect of an information system. Your teacher may ask you to submit a written report or might get you to demonstrate your understanding by questioning you orally.

2.1 Purpose, range and types of users of the information system

2.2 Implementation (hardware and software requirements, storage and connectivity)

2.3 Security risks and safety precautions

2.4 Legal implications

2.5 Impact on the environment.

The type of user of the system must be considered in your write-up. For example, if the information system is for a young or inexperienced user, then the interface should be graphical and free of keyboard commands which are difficult to remember.

The main issues to consider for the hardware and software requirements are the type and speed of the processor, the amount of RAM, the hard disc capacity and the operating system that the information system will run on.

Security risks will include a discussion of how vulnerable the information system is to hacking and virus attacks. You must also mention what steps can be taken to guard against these risks, such as anti-virus software, firewalls, passwords and encryption.

You can find more information on these issues in the 'Security Risks 1', 'Security Risks 2' and 'Security Precautions' spreads in this book.

The main laws to consider are the Data Protection Act (1984), the Computer Misuse Act and the Copyright, Designs and Patents Act. There might be health-and-safety legal issues as well. You can find details on these Acts in the 'Legal Implications' spread in this book.

For the impact on the environment, you should write about the energy consumed by the computers running the software and about the carbon footprint.

 THINGS TO DO AND THINK ABOUT

You must achieve the learning outcomes for the unit assessments by yourself. However, you should take opportunities to seek advice from your teacher on how to proceed with the assessment tasks. Never expect the teacher to complete a task for you; but you can certainly ask for guidance and feedback on your progress.

QUESTIONS AND ANSWERS 1

INTRODUCTION

The following questions are based on the work of the Information System Design and Development unit. They are intended to be similar to the level and style of questions that you can expect in the exam.

QUESTION 1

Mr Strictly works as a teacher in Southton High School. He keeps his student exam marks as a percentage in a database. Ten of the records are shown below.

Student	Form Class	English	Maths	Science	French
Mandy Metcalf	4C	66	50	45	35
Zack Greer	4A	56	70	67	78
Walter Winters	4C	70	78	88	76
Lilly Porter	4D	56	36	41	42
Sophie King	4D	33	67	54	57
Andrew Green	4B	87	35	66	66
Dianna Davidson	4C	57	51	56	52
Ronald Aston	4A	80	68	80	88
Heather Carson	4C	73	83	75	29
Tom Paterson	4A	56	40	55	64

(a) How many fields are there in this database?

(b) Name a field that would be suitable for a range check and describe how the range check would operate.

(c) Name a field that would be suitable for a length check and describe how the length check would operate.

(d) Mr Strictly wants to insert a field to store the average mark for each of the students.

Describe how the database can be used to automatically produce the average marks.

Marks 1, 2, 2, 2

QUESTION 2

A company that sells children's shoes online keeps a relational database of its shoe stock and orders. A stock table and an order table from the database are shown here.

(a) Name the primary field in each table.

(b) Describe the relationship between the tables indicated by the joining lines.

(c) Explain why the Leather Yes/No field in the stock table is a Boolean field.

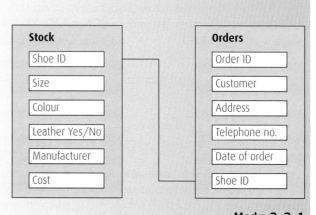

Marks 2, 2, 1

QUESTION 3

A company called Party Fun sells and hires out fancy-dress costumes, masks and tricks on their website. The URL for a web page displaying celebrity masks is shown below.

http://www.partyfun.co.uk/masks/celebrities.htm

| A | B | C | D |

Describe the component parts A, B, C and D of the URL.

Marks 4

QUESTION 4

Sophie is doing a history project about the Second World War. She went on the Internet and found an excellent site that she could use for pictures and sources for her project. Unfortunately, the next day she could not find the website again using a search engine and couldn't remember the website address.

(a) Apart from using a search engine, how could Sophie find the website again?

(b) What should Sophie do in the future to prevent this sort of problem happening again?

Marks 1, 1

ANSWER TO QUESTION 1

(a) There are 6 fields in the database.

(b) The English, Maths, Science or French fields would all be suitable for a range check because they contain data that is a percentage mark. This would mean that any data entered into this field would be validated to be in the range 0 to 100.

(c) The Form Class field is suitable for a length check because it contains data that is always two characters long. This would mean that any data entered into this field would be validated to be exactly two characters.

(d) A calculated field is inserted into the records, which is a field whose data is automatically calculated from other fields within the record. The formula for the calculated field would be = ([English] + [Maths] + [Science] + [French]) / 4

ANSWER TO QUESTION 2

(a) In the Stock table, the primary field is Shoe ID.

In the Orders table, the primary field is Order ID.

(b) This is a one-to-many relationship, since one kind of shoe will appear in many order records. The Shoe ID field in the Stock table is related to many Shoe ID fields in the records of the Order table.

(c) The Leather Yes/No field contains only two values, which are Yes and No. A Boolean field is the correct field type for this purpose.

ANSWER TO QUESTION 3

A The protocol (Hypertext Transfer Protocol) used to transfer the web page.

B The domain name, which is the address of the server computer that is hosting the web page.

C The pathway or route to the page.

D The filename of the file that is being accessed.

ANSWER TO QUESTION 4

(a) Sophie could look at the history in her browser, which keeps a track of previously visited websites.

(b) She could save the website as a bookmark or favourite, which would allow her to go straight to the website with one click.

QUESTIONS AND ANSWERS 2

QUESTION 1

Computers are used by experienced and highly technical users but also by young and inexperienced users.

(a) Why do software packages that use a WIMP user interface also provide keyboard shortcuts?

(b) Tablet computers use a touchscreen for user input. Describe an advantage and a disadvantage of this type of input compared to a keyboard and mouse.

(c) Describe two ways in which the user interface can be designed to make it suitable for a disabled user.

Marks 2, 2, 2

QUESTION 2

Kyle has created a story for the school website on his home computer using a word-processing program that is different from the one that he uses at school.

The school computer will not open the word-processing file that he created on his home computer.

(a) Explain how a standard file format can solve this problem.

(b) Name two possible standard file formats that Kyle could use.

(c) State which of the two file formats would be more suitable, and give a reason for your answer.

Marks 1, 2, 2

QUESTION 3

Wendy is a student in Graymore High School. She has been asked to create two black-and-white bit-mapped graphics for her Art coursework.

(a) Calculate the storage requirement of each graphic in kilobytes.

(i)   480 pixels

600 pixels

(ii)   1,800 pixels

960 pixels

(b) Wendy goes on the Internet to buy a USB flash drive to store a copy of these two files. She finds four devices, shown in the table alongside. State which device you think Wendy should buy, and justify your answer.

(c) Wendy creates a high-resolution and high-bit-depth graphic for the front cover of the program for the school sports. She saves the file and notices that it has a high capacity of 6·2 Mb. Describe two ways in which she can reduce the file size without cropping or changing the size of the image.

Capacity	Cost
8 GB	£6·95
16 GB	£10·95
32 GB	£16·50
64 GB	£53·00

contd

(d) Describe two differences between the BMP and PNG standard file formats for graphics.

Marks 4, 2, 2, 2

QUESTION 4

HTML and JavaScript are both used in the creation of websites.

A website is required to enter the date of birth of the user and then display their star sign (Aquarius, Pisces, Aries etc.).

(a) Explain why JavaScript is required in addition to HTML to perform this function.

(b) A spreadsheet package provides a scripting language facility for the advanced user. Give two ways in which a scripting language can be used by an advanced user.

(c) Describe how a non-expert user with little technical knowledge could make use of a macro to increase their productivity.

Marks 2, 2

ANSWER TO QUESTION 4

(a) HTML uses tags to create a description of the web page by identifying elements on the page such as a header, title, body, style, font size, image, hyperlinks and so on. However, JavaScript is a scripting language that is used to provide the code that processes the date of birth of the user and then displays the star sign.

(b) The scripting language can be used to write code to perform tasks beyond the features offered by the basic package.
The scripting language can also be used to customise the package and automate tasks.

(c) A macro allows the user to record a series of keyboard strokes and mouse clicks that are required to perform a task. The macro can then be allocated to a keyboard shortcut or icon and played back quickly any time the task is required.

ANSWER TO QUESTION 3

(a) (i) The image contains 480 × 600 = 288,000 pixels.
Each pixel requires 1 bit of storage.
Storage requirements = 288,000 bits = 288,000 / 8 bytes = 36,000 bytes
= 36,000 / 1,024 Kb
= 35.2 Kb.

(ii) The image contains 1,800 × 960 = 1,728,000 pixels.
Each pixel requires 1 bit of storage.
Storage requirements = 1,728,000 bits = 1,728,000 / 8 bytes
= 216,000 bytes
= 216,000 / 1,024 Kb
= 210.9 Kb.

(b) Wendy should buy the cheapest 8 GB memory stick for £6.95.
The total size of the two files is only 246.1 Kb, which is thousands of times smaller than the capacity of the 8 GB drive. Buying a higher-capacity device would be unnecessary and a waste of money.

(c) Wendy could save the file in a lower resolution or reduce the number of colours by lowering the bit depth.

(d) BMP does not use compression, while GIF uses lossless compression. BMP can have a high bit depth of 24 bits, providing over 16 million colours, while GIF is limited to 256 colours.

ANSWER TO QUESTION 2

(a) Kyle could save the file in a standard file format for text, which would be opened by most word-processing programs.

(b) TXT or RTF.

(c) RTF would be the more suitable, because it contains formatting information including font, font size and styles as well as the characters.
A TXT file contains the characters in the document but not any formatting information.

ANSWER TO QUESTION 1

(a) A WIMP user interface is easy to use for novice users, who can explore the pull-down menus and icons with the mouse pointer. However, an experienced user can find a WIMP interface slow and clumsy and would prefer to use keyboard shortcuts which he/she can enter more quickly and more efficiently.

(b) Touchscreens save space by replacing the physical keyboard with a pop-up keyboard that appears on the screen; however, most people would find it slower to enter data compared to a traditional keyboard and mouse.

(c) Voice recognition can be used for people who do not have the use of their limbs.
Icons and the font size of text in menus can be made larger for people with poor eyesight.

QUESTIONS AND ANSWERS 3

QUESTION 1

Desktop and laptop computers have a backing store device as well as main memory.

(a) Why do computers require a backing store device when they have main memory to store program and data files while they are being executed?

(b) Desktop computers usually have a hard disc drive as their main backing store device, while laptops have a solid-state drive.
Give an advantage and a disadvantage of a laptop computer using a solid-state drive instead of a hard disc drive.

(c) Name a device that can be used to keep backup copies of the data stored on a computer, and give two reasons why it is a suitable device.

Marks 1, 2, 3

QUESTION 2

Desktop, laptop and tablet are three types of computer.

Given below is a brief description of the computing needs of three people doing different jobs. For each person, state which type of computer is the most suitable, and justify your answer.

A   Sophie is a journalist for a national newspaper who uses a computer to send in her articles from locations throughout the country.

B   Freddy is a civil engineer who uses a computer to create a design of a new bridge to be built.

C   Rosie is a retired financial consultant who spends the day meeting friends and wants to use a computer to monitor the price of her stocks and shares on the Internet.

Marks 2, 2, 2

QUESTION 3

A school hockey team wants to capture some images of the team in action to put on the school website.

(a) Name two hardware devices that can be used to capture graphics to be entered into a computer system.

(b) For each device, describe how the resolution is measured.

(c) State which of the two devices is better suited to capturing the images of the hockey team, and justify your answer.

Marks 2, 2, 2

QUESTION 4

An external disc drive is connected to a computer. An interface provides a physical link between the computer and the disc drive and also stores data until the disc drive is ready to deal with it.

Describe another function of an interface.

Marks 2

ANSWER TO QUESTION 1

(a) RAM loses its contents when the power is switched off. Therefore a backing store device is required to store programs and data files permanently.

(b) A solid-state device has a faster access speed than a hard disc drive and is more robust, which is good for a laptop since it is getting moved about. However, it costs more per unit of storage than a hard disc drive.

(c) USB memory stick is probably the best answer. This device has a fairly high capacity (16 GB is typical) and is robust. It also has a fairly high access speed.
Other possible answers are given below.
CD-RW could also be used. It is cheap and has a reasonable capacity of around 700 Mb.
DVD-RW is similar in cost to a CD-RW but is better in that it has a higher capacity (over 4 GB).

ANSWER TO QUESTION 2

A   A laptop computer. She needs the portability of a laptop computer to carry around with her, so a desktop is not suitable. A tablet computer is not very easy to type data into compared to a physical keyboard on a laptop, so it is not really suitable for typing her articles.

B   A desktop computer is best for this type of work. This is because Freddy needs a large screen display to design the bridge and a full-scale physical keyboard and mouse to interact with the software. In this situation, portability is not an issue since he is presumably working in an office or at home.

C   A tablet is suitable for Rosie, since it is very small and portable and she does not require fast keyboard entry of large amounts of data. She can use the touchscreen on the tablet to enter data and select options.

ANSWER TO QUESTION 3

(a) Digital camera. Scanner.

(b) The resolution of a digital camera is measured in megapixels.
The resolution of a scanner is measured in dots per inch (d.p.i.).

(c) A digital camera is best to capture the images, since a scanner requires the existence of a paper photograph of the team to scan. You can't fit a hockey team under the cover of a flatbed scanner!

ANSWER TO QUESTION 4

Another function of an interface is data conversion. Different voltage levels may need to be converted, or serial data converted to parallel data.

QUESTIONS AND ANSWERS 4

QUESTION 1

A college has a computer network for the use of the students, teachers and administration.

(a) Give three reasons why a computer network is beneficial to the college over using stand-alone computers.

(b) Name an item of hardware that must be installed in a computer in order for it to be connected to a computer network.

(c) The college decided to install wireless instead of wired transmission media. Explain why this might not have been a good decision in terms of bandwidth and security.

Marks 3, 1, 2

QUESTION 2

A small accountancy business has 10 computers and is going to connect them together in a peer-to-peer computer network.

(a) Explain why making a backup copy of the data on a peer-to-peer network is not as easy as it would be on a client/server network.

(b) Apart from backing up data, describe two other disadvantages of a peer-to-peer network compared to a client/server network.

(c) The company had considered installing a client/server network instead of a peer-to-peer network.
Name an item of hardware and an item of software that the company would have needed to purchase if they had installed a client/server network instead of a peer-to-peer network.

Marks 2, 2, 2

QUESTION 3

Polly is looking into buying a video-editing software package to edit her holiday videos. She visits a computer store, where she finds a package with suitable editing features, but she is worried that her 6-year-old computer may not be able to run this package.

(a) Give two reasons why her computer may not have the necessary hardware to run this package.

(b) If Polly's computer has the necessary hardware requirements, is it certain that it will be able to run the video-editing package?
Give a reason for your answer.

Marks 2, 2

QUESTION 4

Cloud storage is an alternative to storing data on hard disc drives and other backing store devices.

Explain one advantage and one disadvantage of using cloud storage to store data.

Marks 2

ANSWER TO QUESTION 1

(a) The students can share the same printer from several computers on the network. Stand-alone computers would require each computer to have its own printer or for students to swap computers in order to print.

Internal e-mail can be used to send messages between the computers.

Students can all access centrally stored program and data files that are installed on the network.

(b) The item of hardware is a NIC (Network Interface Card).

(c) Wireless transmission media in general has a lower bandwidth than wired media such as coaxial cable and optical fibre.

Wireless transmissions are not secure because they are broadcast through infra-red waves, which can be easily intercepted.

ANSWER TO QUESTION 2

(a) On a client/server network, the data is stored centrally on a file server, which makes it easy to make a copy of the data. In a peer-to-peer network, the data is stored on separate computers, which means that the data must be backed up from each computer.

(b) There is less security on a peer-to-peer network, since there is no controlled access to files on a file server.

Installing new software needs to be done on each computer, since there is no file server on which to install and allocate software.

(c) The item of hardware is a file-server computer.

The item of software is a network operating system.

ANSWER TO QUESTION 3

(a) Either of the following two answers is correct.

The computer's processor might be the wrong type or not be fast enough.

The computer might not have sufficient RAM to store the program when it is being run.

It might not have enough hard disc space to store the program permanently.

(b) No. The computer still might not be able to run the software package if it does not have a suitable operating system.

ANSWER TO QUESTION 4

Since the data is being accessed remotely from the Internet, the access speed for saving and loading files can take longer than from a local hard disc drive.

Another possible answer is that since the data is being stored on a remote server, then if there is a problem with the server you would not be able to access any data.

QUESTIONS AND ANSWERS 5

QUESTION 1

Sam works as an accountant in the city of Edinburgh. He spends some of his day in meetings, but most of the time he is sitting at his computer for hours on end.

(a) Describe three health issues that may concern Sam about his working conditions.

(b) Describe three steps that Sam's employer can take to reduce his health risks.

(c) The computer that Sam uses at work got infected by a virus despite his company having anti-virus software installed.
How could Sam's computer still get infected despite the anti-virus software?

(d) Explain the difference between a virus and a worm.

Marks 3, 3, 1, 2

QUESTION 2

Phishing is an Internet fraud that is becoming rapidly more prevalent.

(a) What is phishing?

(b) Describe two ways of identifying phishing on the Internet.

(c) How can phishing be used by criminals for identity theft?

(d) Criminals use identity theft to obtain documents such as passports and driving licences.
How can biometrics be used to catch the fraudulent use of these documents?

Marks 1, 2, 1, 1

QUESTION 3

Legislation exists to protect individuals in society against the wrong use of computing technology.

(a) Name three Acts concerned with computing.

(b) Which Act covers each of the following activities?

    A Deleting records on employees who have left the company.

    B Hacking into confidential data stored on a computer system.

    C Downloading music from the Internet.

    D Sending a virus in an e-mail attachment.

    E Printing out the dialogue for *Grease* from a website and selling it on.

    F Keeping a client database secure with passwords.

Marks 3, 6

QUESTION 4

The growth in prevalence of IT equipment has had consequences for the environment.

(a) Explain what is meant by the term 'carbon footprint'.

(b) Explain how the manufacture and use of computers contributes to the carbon footprint.

(c) Apart from the carbon footprint, describe another way in which the growth of computing has a damaging effect on the environment.

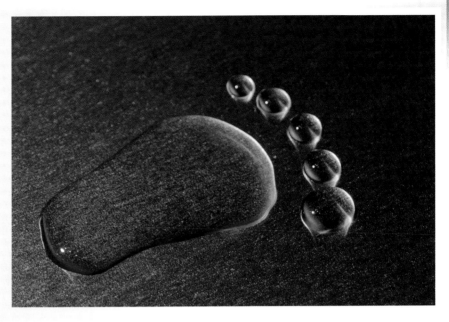

Marks 1, 1, 1

ANSWER TO QUESTION 1

(a) Sam may be concerned about headaches through staring at the computer screen for too long. He may also be worried about back and neck ache through sitting in an uncomfortable position for many hours.
He may also be subject to repetitive strain injury caused by repetitive movement and overuse of muscles brought about by lengthy spells of typing.

(b) The employer can give Sam regular breaks during the day to avoid long periods at the computer.
A screen filter can be put over the screen to diminish the amount of glare.
Comfortable, adjustable seats can be provided to improve Sam's posture.

(c) New viruses are appearing all the time, and the anti-virus software may not be able to recognise the virus.

(d) A virus performs some damaging action such as deleting files or stopping the computer from starting up once infected.
A worm does not specifically perform a damaging action but brings the system to a halt by replicating itself and clogging up the system.

ANSWER TO QUESTION 2

(a) Phishing is the creation of a fraudulent website to trick people into providing their personal data, which can then be used for criminal purposes.

(b) Any two of the following answers would be fine.
The presence of spelling and grammatical errors.
Poor-quality graphics and video.
A poorly designed website with an amateur feel.
Asking you to provide sensitive and private data.
E-mails that are addressed to 'customer', 'client' etc. and not to a specific person.

(c) Fraudulent websites can be used to obtain personal data such as names, addresses, date of birth, nationality and so on that can then be used to obtain important documents under the name of the victim.

(d) Even if a criminal obtains personal data on a victim, they can't forge biometric measurements such as iris and fingerprint scans and voice and face recognition.

ANSWER TO QUESTION 3

(a) Three legal Acts in computing are the Data Protection Act (1984), the Computer Misuse Act (1990) and the Copyright, Designs and Patents Act (1988).

(b) A The Data Protection Act
B The Computer Misuse Act
C The Copyright, Designs and Patents Act
D The Computer Misuse Act
E The Copyright, Designs and Patents Act
F The Data Protection Act

ANSWER TO QUESTION 4

(a) Carbon footprint is a measure of how much carbon dioxide is produced in the making or use of items such as computing devices.

(b) Computing equipment uses electricity, which is produced in power stations by burning fossil fuels such as coal and oil. The waste product of this process is the creation of large amounts of carbon dioxide.

(c) Out-of-date computers are just thrown away, which pollutes the environment with plastic, glass, steel and toxic chemicals such as mercury, lead and cadmium.

COURSE ASSESSMENT

THE COURSEWORK TASK

INTRODUCTION

The course assessment is used to assess your attainment and to provide a grade for the course. The course assessment consists of an exam and a practical assignment. The practical assignment is allocated 60 marks out of a total of 150 for the course assessment. Therefore the practical coursework makes up 40% of the total marks for this course – and a good mark here can go a long way towards overall success.

ONLINE

You can find lots more details on course assessment for National 5 courses from the Scottish Qualifications Authority website at www.brightredbooks.net/N5Computing

THE ASSIGNMENT

You will be given an assignment chosen from a bank of assignments provided by the SQA. Your teacher will choose an assignment that is best suited to your skills and abilities.

The purpose of the assignment is to assess your ability to produce a solution to an appropriate computing problem that is based upon the knowledge and skills that you have developed in the two mandatory units. It is set by the SQA and carried out under controlled conditions. This is an open-book assessment, which means that you can look over programs and information systems that you have previously written to refresh your memory on particular skills that you may have forgotten. You can use manuals and textbooks to get more information and extend your skills.

DON'T FORGET

The course assessment will test your knowledge across both units of the National 5 Computing Science course. If you are unsure of any points, then revise the relevant section in this study guide or ask your teacher for clarification.

Your teacher is allowed to give you some hints and advice – but do not expect him/her to do the assignment for you. You are expected to show your own initiative in this task and to persevere with a problem in the search for a solution. If your teacher gives you significant support with a particular stage of the problem, then he/she will deduct marks for that stage. On the other hand, don't be frightened of asking your teacher for some help if you are completely stuck. At worst, you will lose a mark or two for one part of your solutions, but it will allow you to progress to the next stage, where you can still gain full marks.

The assignment is not just about finding a practical solution at the computer. It involves analysing a problem, designing a solution, implementing the solution and then testing the solution. You should have picked up the necessary skills to address these stages from the work that you have carried out in the unit assessments. The assignment will give guidance in the form of questions, tasks and prompts that will guide you in clear stages through the assessment.

THE REPORT

A word-processed report on the analysis, design, implementation and testing must be provided. Make sure that the report is clear, well presented and free from silly mistakes and spelling and grammatical errors. Have a cover page and appropriate headings and subheadings with consistency in the formatting. Page numbers and headers should be inserted, together with an index page. Avoid using multiple fonts and styles, which would make the document appear cluttered and too 'busy'.

People are impressed by appearances, so don't let your good practical work down by handing in a messy report that is difficult to read.

MARKS

The marks are allocated to the stages of your solution as shown below.

Analysing the problem	10 marks
Designing a solution	10 marks
Implementing a solution	20 marks
Testing the solution	10 marks
Reporting on the solution	10 marks

The assessment is marked internally by the staff in your school according to a strict marking scheme provided by the SQA. This is to make sure that there is a consistency of marking across different schools. To ensure that you get the mark that you deserve for the assignment, quality assurance will be carried out by the SQA. Schools will be asked to provide samples of marked assessments to make sure that the standard of marking is fair.

Evidence

You are expected to provide the following evidence for your coursework assignment.

1 The completed solution in the form of the electronic solution and the written report.

2 A record of progress through the task. This can be in the form of a log giving dates and the tasks completed.

3 A short report on the testing of the solution. This can be done in written or oral form.

 THINGS TO DO AND THINK ABOUT

Take time over your assignment, and make sure that the report is complete and clearly presented. Don't hand in your solution until you are sure that it is completely finished. Your teacher is not allowed to return your assignment for further improvement.

THE EXAM

INTRODUCTION

The course assessment consists of an exam and a practical assignment. The exam is allocated 90 marks out of a total of 150 for the course assessment. Therefore the exam makes up 60% of the total marks for this course. The exam covers the content of the two mandatory units, Software Design and Development and Information System Design and Development.

The exam is set and marked by the SQA and is sat in centres under the exam conditions specified by the SQA.

THE QUESTION PAPER

The question paper has approximately 50% of the marks on each of the two mandatory units.

There are two sections in the question paper.

Section 1   20 marks

This section has short-answer questions that test your knowledge and understanding of the topics listed in the syllabus for each of the mandatory units.

Section 2   70 marks

This section has extended-response questions that test your ability to apply your knowledge and understanding in a challenging problem-solving context.

Total   90 marks

The time allocation for the exam is 1 hour and 30 minutes.

Pace Yourself

The exam has 90 marks that have to be done in 90 minutes, so on average you have 1 minute to do each question. Use this to pace yourself. You want to strike a good balance between finishing the exam in half the time and running out of time halfway through the paper. Finishing the exam in half the time usually means that you have not given fully explained and detailed answers. You should be finishing Section 1 in a little under 20 minutes. Try to leave yourself 5 minutes or so at the end of the exam to check over your answers.

DON'T FORGET

In the exam, ignore the people scribbling at the desks around you, and concentrate on getting your work done in a timely manner. If this means taking a couple of minutes to plan out answers to extended-response questions, then do this!

PREPARATION

There is a specimen paper provided by the SQA to give teachers and students an idea of the kind of questions that they can expect to meet in the actual exam. Your teacher should be able to give you a copy of this paper, or you can download it from the SQA website. It is good preparation to work through this paper, as it will give you a feel for the exam. Also, there are worked answers provided that will give you a good idea of how you are expected to answer the questions.

This, along with past exam papers, will be an invaluable source of revision and will allow you to recognise patterns of questions and topics that come up most frequently. This will allow you to target your revision and improve your chances of success.

You should see this book as an excellent way of consolidating the theory topics covered in class. If you thoroughly learn the contents of this book, then you will have a strong foundation from which to tackle the exam. Remember that you can also use the online Bright Red Digital Zone for extra preparation. Your teacher is also a valuable resource for guidance and preparation. He/she can be a source of extra questions and revision materials or can at least provide information on where to get them for yourself.

ONLINE

The exam timetable is published months before the exams take place in the summer. You can download your own personalised exam timetable from the SQA website.

ONLINE

A great way to revise is to use past papers. You can download these for Computing Science and other subjects online, follow the link at www.brightredbooks. net/N5Computing

THINGS TO DO AND THINK ABOUT

The exam should not come as a surprise to you. If you have carefully studied the contents of this book, then you should have the knowledge required for section 1 and a good foundation to apply the knowledge in the more challenging questions in section 2. Good luck!

GUIDANCE AND ADVICE

INTRODUCTION

This section is here to give you some tips on how you can improve your performance in the practical assignment and the exam. Each of these elements is very important, since they contribute 40% and 60% of the total marks respectively. Remember that you have to pass the learning outcomes for each of the mandatory units to complete the course, but it is your performance in the course assessment in the value-added unit that provides your final grade.

DON'T FORGET

The marking scheme in the exam gives the number of marks awarded to each question. In general, you should make 1 point for 1 mark, 2 points for 2 marks and so on.

READ THE FRONT PAGE

The instructions on the front page of the exam paper give you important information on how to answer the questions. This is the same as the information on the front of the specimen question paper. Save yourself some time in the exam and make sure that you know these instructions before you enter the exam room.

COMMON MISTAKES

It is a mistake made frequently by students to give answers that are too brief and do not give enough explanation or detail.

The example below illustrates this point by giving a good answer and a bad answer to the same question.

EXAMPLE:

Question

The graphic shown below was created with a vector graphics package. Describe how this image is stored by the program.

Good Answer

The image in a vector graphics program is stored as a group of objects together with the attributes of each object. This image would use a rectangle, circle and line object with attributes such as centre x-coordinate, centre y-coordinate, length, breadth, radius, fill colour and so on to describe each shape.

This answer is good because it mentions that vector graphics are stored as objects and attributes and then mentions the actual shapes used in this particular image.

contd

Bad Answer

Different shapes.

This answer gives a hint of what is meant by vector graphics by using the word 'shapes' as opposed to 'pixels' but is far too brief and is not using the appropriate technical terms. Also, there is no description of how vector graphics would store the actual image shown here.

It would have been better to use the word 'objects' rather than 'shapes'. There is no mention that the attributes or features of each object are stored.

It is surprisingly frequent for students to answer their own version of a question rather than the one given in the question paper. This is usually due to not reading the information at the start of the question and then skimming through what is being asked.

Make sure that you read the question properly.

DON'T FORGET

It is always a good idea to put any relevant technical terms into your answers. For example, when describing 'bit-mapped', it is better to use the terms 'pixel' and 'resolution' as opposed to 'dots' and 'detail'.

OUTSIDE THE CLASS

The practical assignment is done under supervised conditions in the classroom. However, there is no problem with you doing preparation work at home. Once you have been given the instructions for the assessment, you should think about which parts you can research or which skills you need to practise more at home. You must write the report in the class, but you can reflect upon what needs to be done and make brief notes at home.

AVOID STRESS

It is very easy to feel stressed in the run-up to the exams. There are steps that you can take to reduce the stress and improve your performance.

Exercise releases tension and takes your mind off the issues that are stressing you. You do not need to run 10 miles. Even a short walk can have a relaxing and calming effect.

Try to make a peaceful study area for yourself which is quiet and free from distractions. It is very hard to study effectively in a family room with a loud TV on and your baby sister tugging your feet!

It is also important that you don't work too hard and overdo it. Studies have shown that relatively short periods of studying, each followed up with a short break, are more effective than working flat out for hours on end.

Remember that what you eat and drink also has an influence on how you feel and on your ability to concentrate. A healthy, well-balanced diet will put you in a much better state of mind for study than if you consume fizzy drinks and junk food.

VIDEO

Watch the clip on tackling assignments: www.brightredbooks.net/N5Computing

ONLINE

The SQA has a study guide section on its website which gives further support on how to prepare for and cope with exams. Enter the keywords 'SQA' and 'study guide' into a search engine to find this information.

 THINGS TO DO AND THINK ABOUT

Each year, the SQA produces an examiner's report, which can be found on its website. This report gives helpful comments on strong and weak areas of student performance and cut-off scores for each grade. This report can give you a useful insight into the exam process.

GLOSSARY

Address bus
A processor bus that is used to specify which memory location is to be used to read data from or to write data to.

Adware
Software that irritatingly displays advertisements on a computer.

ALU (Arithmetic Logic Unit)
A component of the processor that performs arithmetic operations and logical decisions.

And
A logical operator that requires both of two conditions to be true.

Anti-virus software
Software that scans a computer system to detect and remove viruses.

Application package
A program that is used to perform a useful function or solve a problem for the user such as word-processing, stock control, video-editing and so on.

Array
A data structure that stores a list of items of the same data type.

ASCII
American Standard Code for Information Interchange. A system for storing characters on a computer system using an 8-bit code.

Assignment
The process of assigning a value to a variable.

AVI (Audio Video Interleave)
A standard file format for video that does not use compression.

Backing store device
A device used to permanently store data in a computer system.

Bandwidth
A term used to describe the speed of data transfer over a network.

Binary
A two-digit numerical system which computers use to represent data.

Biometrics
A form of security system based on the detection and recognition of human physical characteristics.

Bit
A binary digit (1 or 0).

Bit depth
The number of bits allocated for the colour code of each pixel.

Bit-mapped
A graphic where the image is stored as a binary code for the colour of pixels.

Blu-Ray
A very high-capacity optical disc that is read by a laser with a capacity of 25 GB.

BMP (Bitmap)
A standard file format for graphics that uses a binary code to store the colour of each pixel.

Boolean
A data type used for a variable that is storing only the values True or False.

Boolean field
A field that stores only two values (Yes or No).

Broadband connection
A fast Internet connection that is always on.

Browser
A program that is used to display web pages and navigate around the Internet.

Byte
A group of 8 bits.

Calculation field
A field whose contents are calculated by a formula using the other fields in a record.

Carbon footprint
A measure of how much carbon dioxide is produced in the making and use of computing equipment.

CD (Compact Disc)
An optical disc that is read by a laser with a capacity of 700 Mb.

Client/server network
A large-scale computer network where server computers provide network resources to clients which make use of the resources.

Cloud storage
A type of storage that uses online services to store large amounts of data on the Internet or on a remote computer network.

Coaxial cable
A moderately fast and low-cost electrical transmission medium which is shielded against interference.

Compiler
A translator program which converts high-level language code into stand-alone machine code.

Computer Misuse Act (1990)
An Act which outlaws hacking into computer systems and the sending of viruses to cause harm.

Conditional loop
A loop that repeats a set of instructions as often as is necessary until a condition is true.

Conditional statement
A statement that is either True or False.

Control bus
A processor bus that sends out signals along various lines to initiate events.

Control character
Non-printing characters such as RETURN and TAB.

Control unit
A component of the processor that manages the fetching and execution of instructions from main memory.

Copyright, Designs and Patents Act (1988)
An Act which covers the illegal copying of music, films, images, manuscripts etc. stored on a computer.

CPU (Central Processing Unit)
The part of a computer that executes programs and consists of a processor chip and main memory chips.

CRT (Cathode Ray Tube)
A bulky, old-fashioned monitor that guides a stream of electrons with magnets onto a phosphorescent screen.

CSV (Comma Separated Values)
A standard file format that can be used to save tabular data such as spreadsheets by using symbols to separate the rows and columns.

Database
An organised collection of records.

Data bus
A processor bus that is used to carry data from a memory location to the processor and vice versa.

Data Protection Act (1984)
An Act to protect the rights of individuals in society against misuse of their data being held on computer systems.

Data subjects
The individuals on whom data is kept on databases.

Data types
Different kinds of data stored by a variable in a program, such as Integer, String, Boolean and so on.

Data users
The people who make use of the data held on databases.

Date field
A field that stores a date.

Denial-of-service attack
An attack on a company's network that puts it under pressure in a way that prevents legitimate users from being able to use the network resources.

Desktop computer
A computer that is small enough to sit on a desk but is not easily moved around.

Dial-up connection
A slow Internet connection that requires a connection to be made at the start of each session.

Digital camcorder
An input device for video that captures the data as a series of bit-mapped graphics frames per second.

Digital camera
An input device for graphics that captures millions of dots of light to store an image.

Direct access
Access to data stored on disc which can be read directly from any part of the disc.

Domain name
The address of the server computer that is hosting a web page.

DVD (Digital Versatile Disc)
A high capacity optical disc that is read by a laser with a capacity of 4.7 GB.

Encryption
Encoding data so that it cannot be interpreted if unlawfully accessed.

Exceptional data
A set of test data that is chosen to test whether the software can deal with unexpected data without crashing.

Execution errors
Errors that are detected during the running of the program, such as dividing by zero.

Exponent
The power part of a floating-point number.

Extreme data
A set of test data that is chosen to test that the software can handle data which lies on the boundaries of possible data.

Field
An item of data in a database record.

Firewall
Hardware and software that is used to protect a computer from damage by filtering all incoming and outgoing Internet traffic.

Fixed loop
A loop that repeats a set of instructions a pre-determined number of times.

Flash memory
Solid-state memory such as memory cards and USB memory sticks.

Flat-bed plotter
An output device that draws an image using a pen on a horizontal sheet of paper.

Flat-file database
A database that contains records in only one table of data.

Floating-point notation
A method of storing real numbers on a computer system.

Foreign key
A field that contains values that correspond to values in the primary key of another table.

Frame rates
The number of frames that are captured per second.

GIF (Graphics Interchange Format)
A standard file format for graphics that uses lossless compression and represents 256 colours.

Gigabyte (GB)
A gigabyte = 2^{30} bytes = 1,073,741,824 bytes.

Graphics field
A field that stores an image.

Graphics tablet
An input device that enters graphics by writing on a horizontal surface with a special pen called a stylus.

Hacking
Gaining access to private and confidential data on a computer system.

Hard disc drive
The main storage device of a desktop computer that stores data by using different forms of magnetisation on a disc.

Hardware
The physical parts of a computer such as the keyboard, hard disc drive and so on.

High-level language
A programming language that uses English command words to make the process of software development easier and quicker.

Hotspot
An active area of the screen that initiates an event when the mouse pointer hovers over it.

HTML (Hypertext Mark-up Language)
A language that uses a list of tags to describe a web page's format and what is displayed on the page.

HTTPS (Hypertext Transfer Protocol Secure)
A protocol used by organisations, such as banks and companies involved in e-commerce, on their websites to transfer data securely over the Internet.

Hyperlink
A link in an information system to another item within the file or to a document outside the file.

Identity theft
Stealing your identity by finding out your personal details on computer systems.

Indentation
Indenting instructions in the program code to make it easier to identify selection, looping and so on.

Inkjet printer
A printer that works by spraying thousands of tiny droplets of quick-drying ink onto paper as it is fed through the printer.

Input device
A device used to enter data into a computer system.

Input validation
The process of repeatedly asking for an item of data to be entered until it is within its possible range of values.

Integer
A data type used for a variable that is storing a positive or negative whole number.

Interface
A link between a peripheral device and the CPU that compensates for differences in how they operate.

Internal commentary
Comments inserted into a program listing to explain what the instructions are doing.

Internet
A global computer network that consists of LANs and individual computers all connected up together.

Interpreter
A translator program which converts high-level language code into machine code one instruction at a time when the program is run.

ISP (Internet Service Provider)
A company that provides a connection to the Internet and allows the user to be online.

Iteration
The process where programs repeat a group of instructions two or more times.

JavaScript
A programming language that can be incorporated into web pages to add interactivity and make them more dynamic.

Joystick
A stick that can be moved in different directions to control the movement of an object on the screen with a button which is used as a trigger.

JPEG (Joint Photographic Enterprise Group)
A standard file format for graphics that uses lossy compression and represents over 16 million colours.

Key field
A field that uniquely identifies a record in a database.

Keylogger
Software that records the keys that the user presses on a computer keyboard.

Kilobyte (Kb)
A kilobyte = 2^{10} bytes = 1,024 bytes.

LAN (Local Area Network)
A computer network that is located in a relatively small area such as a school or an office where the computers are linked by cables or wireless connections.

Laptop computer
A computer that is portable and suitable for use on the go.

Laser printer
A printer that uses toner powder which sticks to electrically charged areas of a cylindrical drum to transfer an image to paper.

LCD (Liquid Crystal Display)
A low-power type of flat screen that charges crystals to produce the image.

Logical errors
Errors caused by mistakes in the code that cause the program not to produce the correct results.

Lossless compression
File compression that results in no reduction in quality.

Lossy compression
File compression that reduces the quality of the file.

Loudspeaker
An output device used in conjunction with a sound card to create sound.

Machine code
The computer's own programming language where instructions and data are written in binary codes.

Magnetic tape drive
A storage device that stores data by using different forms of magnetisation on a tape.

Main memory
Memory in the CPU that is used to store programs temporarily while they are being run.

Mantissa
The fractional part of a floating-point number which stores the significant figures of the number.

Meaningful identifiers
Variable names that relate to the data that the variable is storing.

Megabyte (Mb)
A megabyte = 2^{20} bytes = 1,048,756 bytes.

Microphone
An input device used in conjunction with a sound card to capture sound.

Mouse
An input device used to move a pointer and select options on the screen.

MP3 (MPEG Layer 3)
A standard file format for sound that uses lossy compression so that the quality is reduced.

MPEG (Motion Picture Experts Group)
A standard file format for video that uses lossy compression.

Multimedia
A combination of text, graphics, video and sound data.

Nested loop
A loop which is placed completely inside another loop.

Networked computer
A computer that is connected to one or more other computers.

Normal data
A set of test data that is chosen to test that the software gives correct results for everyday data.

Not
A logical operator that switches a statement that is False to a statement that is True and vice versa.

Numeric field
A field that stores a number.

Online fraud
Schemes that use the Internet to unlawfully obtain money and property.

Operating system
A large program that manages the hardware and software of a computing system.

Optical fibre
A high-bandwidth transmission medium that is used to transfer high volumes of data and which is very unsusceptible to interference.

Or
A logical operator that requires one of two conditions to be true.

Output device
A device used to show the results of processing on a computer system.

PDF (Portable Document Format)
A file format that captures text, fonts, images and formatting of documents from a variety of applications.

Peer-to-peer network
A cheap, small-scale computer network used for a small number of computers in a trusted environment.

Peripheral
An input, output or storage device that is connected to the CPU.

Petabyte (Pb)
A petabyte = 2^{50} bytes = 1,125,899,906,842,624 bytes.

Phishing
The process of stealing private information through using false websites.

Pixel
A picture element; one of the tiny dots that make up a picture.

PNG (Portable Network Graphics)
A standard file format for graphics that uses lossless compression and represents over 16 million colours.

Pre-defined function
A function built into the programming language which performs mathematical calculations, manipulates text and so on.

Primary key
A field that is used to uniquely identify each record in a table.

Protocol
An agreed set of rules between a sender and a receiver to ensure successful communication.

Pseudocode
A method of design that uses natural language to represent the detailed logic of the program code.

QWERTY
A keyboard with the first six letters on the top left corner of the keyboard spelling QWERTY.

RAM (Random-Access Memory)
Part of main memory that can be read from and written to.

Random access
Another term for direct access (see 'Direct access').

Readable
Program code that is easily understood by another programmer.

Real
A data type used for a variable that is storing a positive or negative decimal number.

Record
Data on one person, animal or object in a database that consists of several fields.

Registers
Individual storage locations on the processor that store single items of data.

Relational database
A database that contains records in two or more linked tables.

Resolution
The size of the pixels in an image, usually described in dots per inch (d.p.i.).

ROM (Read-Only Memory)
Part of main memory that can be read from but not written to.

RTF (Rich Text Format)
A standard file format for text that contains formatting information including font, font size and styles such as bold and underline.

Sample size
The number of bits used to store each sound sample.

Sampling rate
The number of times that the sound is sampled per second.

Scanner
An input device that for graphics that scans an image on paper and enters it into a computer system.

Scripting language
A language that operates alongside an application package and allows the user to customise the package and to automate tasks.

Search engine
A program that locates websites based upon keywords and phrases entered by the user.

Searching
Selecting records in a database according to certain rules based on one or more fields.

Security protocol
An agreement between a sender and a receiver about how data is sent so that a successful and secure exchange can take place.

Security suite
A group of utility programs that protect a computer from viruses and other malware.

Selection
A programming construct where different sets of instructions are chosen to allow the program to make decisions.

Sequencing
A programming construct where the instructions are executed one after another.

Sequential access
Access to data stored on tape in which other data must be read through to get to the target data.

Smartphone
A mobile phone that includes functions beyond making calls and texting that are traditionally associated with a computer.

Software
Computer programs such as Windows, Excel and so on.

Solid-state
A backing store device with no moving parts, such as flash memory.

Sorting
Arranging the records in a database into ascending or descending order.

Spyware
Software that, once installed on your computer, can 'spy' on your activities.

Stand-alone computer
A computer that is not connected to any other computer.

Standard algorithms
Common algorithms that are used in programs over and over again.

Standard file format
A file format that is recognised by a variety of software packages.

Stepwise refinement
A series of steps in which a large problem is broken down into parts and then those parts themselves are further broken down into smaller parts.

Storage device
A device used to keep a permanent copy of program and data files when the computer is switched off.

String
A data type used for a variable that is storing an item of text.

Structure diagram
A method of design that splits a program up into successively smaller and more manageable parts in a hierarchical structure.

Supercomputer
A very powerful computer that has an extremely high processing speed and massive storage capacity.

Syntax errors
Errors which result from mistakes in the instructions of a programming language.

Tablet computer
A flat portable computer that is larger than a smartphone and smaller than a laptop, which uses a touchscreen for input rather than a physical keyboard.

Tags
Commands that are used to describe a web page by identifying elements on the page such as a header, title, body and so on.

Terabyte (Tb)
A terabyte = 2^{40} bytes = 1,099,511,627,776 bytes.

Test data
Sets of data chosen to detect and remove errors in a program.

Text field
A field that stores a string of characters.

TFT (Thin Film Transistor)
A type of flat-screen display which is made up of very small transistors.

Time field
A field that stores a time of day.

Touchpad
An input device which uses your finger on a small pad to move the pointer and make selections.

Touchscreen
A screen that accepts input by detecting human touch on an electronic grid.

Transmission media
The cabling or wireless connection that is used to link computers on a network.

Trojan
Software that masquerades as a legitimate program and creates a 'back door' on a computer that gives malicious users access to the files stored on the computer.

Two-state
A system that has only two states, for example a switch that is off or on.

Two's complement
A system for storing integers on a computer system.

TXT (Text)
A standard file format for text that stores no formatting information.

Uniform Resource Locator
A unique address that specifies a web page by the protocol, the domain name, the path to the file and the name of the file.

Unshielded Twisted Pair (UTP)
A low-cost but low-bandwidth electrical transmission medium which is not shielded against interference.

User interface
A term used to describe how the user communicates with a computer program.

Utility
Software that adds functionality or helps in the maintenance of a computer system.

Variable
A label for an item of data that is stored in a program.

Vector graphics
A graphic where the image is stored as a list of objects and their attributes.

Video conferencing
A virtual conference which uses online computers and multimedia hardware devices.

Virus
A program which causes damage to a computer system and can replicate and spread to other computers.

WAV (Waveform Audio Format)
A standard file format for sound that uses lossless compression.

WIMP (Windows, Icons, Menus, Pointer)
A type of interface in which the mouse or another pointing device is used to select choices on pull-down menus and icons.

World Wide Web (WWW)
The vast amount of multimedia information stored on websites on server computers on the Internet.

Worm
A program which replicates itself to the extent that it clogs up the system and spreads automatically from computer to computer.

XLS (Excel file extension)
The file extension for Microsoft Excel spreadsheet files.

XML (Extensible Mark-up Language)
A standard file format commonly used with HTML documents that can be used to store spreadsheet files.